THE ORGANIZED WEDDING:

PLANNING EVERYTHING FROM YOUR ENGAGEMENT TO YOUR MARRIAGE

LIZ LONG

Cover Photo courtesy of My Vintage Vogue.

www.MyVintageVogue.com

 Two Crazy Boys Publishing.

ISBN: 0984954260

ISBN-13: 978-0984954261

DEDICATION

To my beloved husband.

Table of Contents

ACKNOWLEDGMENTS

Thank you to my husband for his support and encouragement in writing this, and to my children for their tolerance while I edited this. Without them, this book certainly wouldn't exist.

Foreword

Dear Reader:

When my husband and I got married, I spent a year planning our wedding. It was attended by 150 of our friends and relatives, and our parents' friends and co-workers[1]. Our wedding day was lots of fun, but it took lots of work to pull it all together.

When we got engaged, my husband and I knew some of what was required to plan a wedding ceremony, reception and honeymoon, but we needed to learn a lot more. Some of it was in the wedding planners we found but a lot wasn't, especially for the ceremony and honeymoon. Those books were also too heavy and bulky to carry with us while we planned the biggest party of our lives, and too floral to leave out at work.

This planner provides a lot of information, hopefully without overwhelming you. It's organized it so you can find everything quickly. To achieve all this, each section has a short

---

[1] Meeting new people (often your parents' co-workers and relatives you thought died years ago) at your wedding is so common it should be considered a tradition. Be prepared for a long list of people your parents are sure "must be" invited but that you don't know. Just try to convince them to limit it and accept meeting some new people. If they weren't proud of you, they wouldn't want their entire office at your wedding.

introduction followed by hints and tips for saving time and money, then by checklists to help you take care of all the important details.

There are even recommendations for home security precautions during your honeymoon. It's easy to forget to have a friend pick up packages (wedding gifts!) from USPS, FedEx and UPS or forward / hold packages so they aren't returned to sender.

We had a Protestant ceremony, but this book doesn't assume that you will. That is why we refer to your "officiant" – not pastor, priest, rabbi, or judge – and "ceremony site" – not church, synagogue, or courthouse. Although there will clearly be differences depending on your religion, many things are similar for any type of wedding. For example, if you have a religious officiant, you will probably need to be counseled before they will marry you. You will also need to select appropriate (non-secular) ceremony music (not just the processional and recessional) and readings.

Compromise is integral to planning a wedding, especially if someone else is paying for it. While it is *your* wedding, you will still need to consider other people's wishes, budgetary and dietary restrictions, and both sets of family traditions. When you start planning, ask each set of parents if there is anything they strongly feel should be included in your wedding and include it, if possible.

You and your fiancé should decide what you feel

strongly about and tell your families that you won't compromise on those items. Parents can feel that they have the right to make all the major decisions, especially if they pay for everything, potentially making it more difficult to get *your* dream wedding instead of *their* dream wedding.

Most importantly, remember that although you do need to consider other people, it is ***your*** wedding. Do what is most important to the two of you. Don't let a bossy photographer cut short your dinner because the lighting is "just right" outside if food is important to you. And don't let a caterer intimidate you into finishing dinner and missing the "perfect lighting" if photos are very important to you. And if you love chocolate cake, get a double-double chocolate cake with fudge frosting. Just don't drop it on the bride's gown. (You can always get a white groom's cake.)

Try to remember that even if they deliver the wrong cake, the limo driver is a no-show, there's a monsoon, and the band plays music you hate, *you will still have just married the person of your dreams!!!*

Isn't that what the whole thing is really about?

Wishing you all the best,

Liz Long

Glossary

Bride's Cake: The traditional white, layered cake. It no longer "has to be" either white, which doesn't rise well, or layered.

Bridesmaid's Luncheon: A small celebration in honor of your bridesmaids and all the help they've given you. Both mothers are invited. A trip to a day spa is a popular alternative.

Bulletin/Program: Handed out at the ceremony, they list the attendants and family, ceremony order, and any special notes from the couple.

Cash Bar: Your guests pay for all or most of their drinks. You can also provide one drink (e.g., margaritas or beer) and have guests pay for everything else. See Open Bar.

Groom's Cake: A smaller cake in a shape or flavor reflecting the groom's interests (e.g., a golf scene or fraternity letters). Definitely optional.

Honor Attendant: For the bride, the maid or matron of honor. For the groom, the best man.

Host/Hostess: The person you designate to handle any problems during the wedding and reception. This may be one of your parents.

Officiant: The person who marries you. This can be a pastor, priest, rabbi, judge, "Chapel of Love" owner, or any other person recognized by the state you are marrying in.

Open Bar: You pay for everything your guests drink. See Cash Bar.

Processional: Music played as the bride and her attendants go down the aisle.

Receiving Line: The couple and their parents greet each guest as they walk through a line. It can take a long time, but may be the only chance to talk to some guests. May include honor attendants.

Recessional: Music played as the new couple and their attendants go back the aisle.

Registry: A gift wish list. The couple selects a few stores with registries, then spends several hours selecting the dishes, towels, picture frames, etc. they want to use for the next few decades. Have fun!

Rehearsal Dinner: Usually held after the rehearsal, all ceremony participants and out-of-town guests who have arrived are invited. Invitations are informal and attendants' gifts may be given out here. This can be a formal dinner or a barbecue - whatever you want.

Response Cards: Pre-addressed cards stamped and mailed in your wedding invitations. Guests write their name on the card inside and indicate if they will be attending and how many will be in their party. For sit-down meals, guests also indicate which menu choice they prefer.

Stationery: The paper products needed for a wedding - invitations, response cards, personalized napkins/matchbooks, and so much more!

Table Assignments: An exceptionally painful process, this is when you decide who will sit next to whom at the reception. The advantage is that you can make certain that your friends are at the same table, not with your parents' coworkers. The disadvantage is that it takes time. If you have table assignments, you need to have place cards and a place card table. It's usually worth the effort, but check with both sets of parents to find out which feuding relatives should be separated.

Thermography: Engraving was the standard for wedding invitations. Today, thermography successfully imitates the appearance of engraving for a lot less money.

Toss Bouquet: Instead of throwing the expensive bouquet they have put so much time and money into, brides may buy a toss bouquet. It is a much smaller version of her bouquet. Of course, some brides skip the toss altogether, but both the bouquet and garter toss are fun for kids.

Ushers: Usually men, they escort guests to their seat prior to the wedding ceremony. Groomsmen are often the ushers too. You should have one usher for every 50 guests.[2]

[2] Note: The following items are only used in Jewish weddings: Huppot and poles, Kiddush cup, Ketubah, Yarmulkes, Kittel, and glasses to break.

Superstitions and Traditions

- .. Something old, something new, something borrowed, and something blue, and a silver sixpence in your shoe. This tradition dates from the late 1900s.
- .. It's bad luck for the groom to see the bride before their wedding on their wedding day. (Personally, I think this is because the soon-to-be-married are often quite tense and could start arguing over nothing and ruin their wedding.) This is a Victorian tradition.
- .. It's bad luck to receive a knife as a gift. Include a penny as payment in thank you notes for knives.
- .. First time (and only first time) brides must wear white. Brides started wearing white in the eighteenth century, but it wasn't until the Victorian era that a "white wedding" became de rigeur.
- .. Attendants dress alike to confuse evil spirits. Thousands of years old.
- .. Rice is thrown to buy off cranky spirits. Hundreds of years old.
- .. Wedding rings are worn on the ring finger of the left hand because the vein in this finger was believed to go directly to the heart. Thousands of years old.

Notes

Key Telephone Numbers

☐ ..... Baby-sitter ____________________

☐ ..... Baker ____________________

☐ ..... Band/DJ ____________________

☐ ..... Best Man ____________________

☐ ..... Bridal store/alteration shop ____________________

☐ ..... Bridesmaids' gown store ____________________

☐ ..... Caterer ____________________

☐ ..... Ceremony site ____________________

☐ ..... County Clerk (for marriage license) ____________________

☐☐. Doctor (general practitioner) ____________________

☐ ..... Florist ____________________

☐ ..... Hair stylist ____________________

☐ ..... Honeymoon hotel ____________________

☐ ..... Hotel for out-of-town guests ____________________

☐ ..... Jeweler ____________________

☐ ..... Limo company ____________________

☐ ..... Maid of Honor ____________________

☐ ..... Make-up artist ____________________

☐ ..... Manicurist ____________________

☐ ..... OB/Gyn ____________________

- [ ] ...... Officiant ______________________
- [ ] ...... Organist/other musician ______________________
- [ ] ...... Parents - Hers ______________________
- [ ] ...... Parents - His ______________________
- [ ] ...... Pet kennel ______________________
- [ ] ...... Photographer ______________________
- [ ] ...... Reception site ______________________
- [ ] ...... Registry #1 ______________________

  Registry Number ______________________
- [ ] ...... Registry #2 ______________________

  Registry Number ______________________
- [ ] ...... Rental company (tables, etc.) ______________________
- [ ] ...... Rehearsal dinner location ______________________
- [ ] ...... Soloist ______________________
- [ ] ...... Travel agent ______________________
- [ ] ...... Tuxedo rental ______________________
- [ ] ...... Videographer ______________________
- [ ] ...... Wedding coordinator ______________________
- [ ] ...... Wedding night hotel ______________________

Basic Information

Try to make the major decisions, including vendors, at least nine months before your wedding. Most of the good ones book up at least that far in advance. Finish everything that can be done in advance by two months before your wedding. Obviously, some things (table assignments, packing) can't be done until just before the wedding but if you get everything else done in advance, you'll be able to fully enjoy the last weeks before your wedding.

There are a few things you should do one year in advance to find in-season items. Most importantly, as soon as you decide your colors, both your mothers should start shopping for their dresses. The Bride's mother chooses her gown first, then the Groom's mother coordinates with her dress. The mothers should discuss the colors and styles they want to wear so they coordinate.

There are several To-Do Lists for specific people. One is for the Groom and includes the things they traditionally do. The other two are for the Bride and Groom's mothers. They are totally blank, beyond choosing a dress. You need to figure out what you are comfortable having them do. They want to make sure everything goes perfectly, and they want to be involved in the planning. They might even know a few things that are helpful for you. If you select areas that you want their help in, and are clear about areas that you and your fiancé want to decide yourselves, hopefully it will reduce some tension.

Since my Mom is a church organist, she was in charge of selecting an organist. As I told her, I had no opinion on that subject – it was her call. If you let your mothers help in areas they care (or know) about more than you do, they might stop trying to "help" in areas where you really don't want it. It can also free up some of your time to devote to things you care about more. When they start really bugging you, remember that they have been dreaming about (or possibly dreading) this day since before you were born. Whichever it was, they just want it to be perfect.

If your fiancé is not involved enough with planning your wedding, you might be overwhelming them with details. (Hasn't the whole process occasionally overwhelmed you?) Don't ask about things you know they *really* won't care about. My husband didn't know when we ordered a cake knife set, much less care what it looked like.

For areas you truly need help with, try narrowing the options and giving them three you like so they can't pick the wrong one. For example, I couldn't decide between two processional songs I loved so my husband chose.

When most people think of a wedding party, they think of the maid/matron of honor, bridesmaids, groomsmen, flower girl, ring bearer, bride and groom. In addition to these people, you can include Junior Bridesmaids, Junior Groomsmen, and ushers who are not groomsmen. Groomsmen stand up front during the ceremony. Ushers seat people. Groomsmen are often ushers too, but it's up to you. (As a rule of thumb, you should have one usher for every fifty guests.) Both sets of parents are also part of the bridal party.

Aside from the wedding party, you can ask friends to help with your wedding in a variety of ways. Examples include a guest book attendant, acolyte, reader and Huppot pole bearer. Although these people are not technically part of the Wedding Party (and therefore get out of the multi-hour photo shoots), they do help things run more smoothly.

There is a lot of information your wedding party needs to have. In fact, there's an entire checklist devoted to just this. There's a second checklist to remind you to send the information to everyone who needs it. You should also give everyone in your bridal party a list of exactly what you expect them to do in your wedding. Don't assume they know it all.

There are pages reminding you to record what you bought for each person as a thank-you gift and how much you paid. This will help to jog your memory so that you don't inadvertently spend a lot more/less on one person.

Hints and Tips

- If you live in or near a city with a central flower market, go look at their flowers. You may find new ones that you love for your wedding. Try to look 12 months ahead to find in-season flowers.
- If you live in or near a city with a garment district, look for a headpiece and veil there. It's less expensive.
- If you need something on your wedding day, ask someone for help. It might take you 20 minutes to get a glass of water, or a guest could bring it to you in two minutes. Most people will understand and be glad to help.
- Possible ways to limit the guest list include not having children (under 16 or 18?), coworkers, dates for single guests, or distant relatives.
- Before mailing response cards, write the guest's name on the back (or number the guest list and put the corresponding number) so you know who is responding, even if they forget to write their name.
- If you find a vintage gown that's a little tight, try a bustier/corset. Custom ones can suck you in where the gown is tight. This can be very cost effective compared to buying a new gown.
- You will be showing off your engagement and wedding rings on your wedding day. You can have a jeweler clean your engagement ring just

before your wedding. You can also buy a small high-quality brush and use dish-detergent to clean it yourself in five minutes. (This recommendation is from a jeweler.)

- Your Honor Attendants (Maid/Matron of Honor and Best Man) should be at least 21 years old because they are the legal witnesses who sign your marriage certificate. Alternatively, you may designate another attendant to serve as your official witness.
- Your attendants and anyone else who is particularly helpful with your wedding is usually given a thank-you gift.

Considerations for setting a date:

- The peak season for weddings is April through October, causing intense competition for resources.
- What is your favorite season? What special dates do the two of you have?
- Does either family already have any conflicting events planned – trips, reunions, graduations?
- Avoid busy-season at work, because it will always be busy-season on your anniversary.
- Consider how heavy travel days and holidays will impact guests who live far away.

Newspaper Announcements:

- Review it before publication.
- Usually made by the parents of the bride not more than one year in advance.
- Gives the couple's names, their parent's names and the wedding date. May also ask where they were educated/degrees received, where they live, and current occupation and employer.
- Usually sent to the lifestyle or society editor of the local paper. A fee may be charged to print it.

Registering

- If you register more than six months in advance, items may be discontinued or you may select seasonal items your guests won't be able to find.
- Select two or three stores and register before your first shower. It's a good idea to make sure at least one is a national chain.
- Make sure the stores have branches convenient to your guests. Check return/exchange policies.
- You can register for more than dishes and linens. Power drills, mortgages, and more are available on registries. Include a few expensive gifts for groups who pool their money to buy a large gift.
- Include inexpensive items too. There are some really good slotted spoons, pizza cutters, etc. available. Each item is only a few dollars, but a

full set can be costly.

- Tell your family and attendants where you register. They tell everyone else. Do not put this information in shower or wedding invitations.
- There is a multi-page gift recorder at the end of this book for your wedding gifts. When you open the bulk of your gifts after your wedding, have a few friends over for a small party. That way, they can record who gave you what as you open your gifts.

Bridal Shower:

- Held at least two weeks before your wedding. Informal, they can be co-ed and may have a theme (barbecue, kitchen, lingerie, linen).
- The bride is often involved in scheduling her shower. You may have several.
- You will need a gift recorder. Have an attendant or other friend record who gave you what in the "Engagement and Shower Gift Recorder" at the end of this book, or on a pad of paper.
- **If guests attend multiple showers, they are not expected to give multiple gifts.**
- Even if the shower is at your parents' home, they should not be the official hosts. Your honor attendant should be.

Notes

Budget

Bride's Priorities

Think about what **really** matters to you and number this list accordingly. It should help you figure out the budget and where other people can "help."

☐ ..... Ceremony Site ____________________

- ☐ ...... Unity Candle ____________________
- ☐ ...... Huppot, Kiddush Cup ____________

☐ ..... Musician(s):

- ☐ ...... Soloist ____________________
- ☐ ...... Ceremony Musician(s) ____________
- ☐ ...... Reception Band/DJ ____________

☐ ..... Photographer ____________________

☐ ..... Videographer ____________________

☐☐. Bachelorette Party/Bridesmaids Lunch _____

☐ ..... Rehearsal Dinner ____________________

☐ ..... Reception Site ____________________

☐ ..... Food & Beverages:

- ☐ ...... Appetizers ____________________
- ☐ ...... Entrees ____________________
- ☐☐. Cake (primary, Groom's) __________
- ☐ ...... Drinks/Bar ____________________

☐ ..... Rental items (tables, chairs, etc.) __________

- [ ] ...... Favors ____________________
- [ ] ...... Guest Book ____________________
- [ ] ...... Bird seed/Bubbles ____________________
- [ ] ...... Invitations ____________________
    - [ ] ......Calligraphy ____________________
- [ ] ...... Limousine ____________________
- [ ] ...... Flowers:
    - [ ] ......Bridal Bouquet ____________________
    - [ ] ......Attendants ____________________
    - [ ] ......Parents/Special Guests ____________________
    - [ ] ......Ceremony Site ____________________
    - [ ] ......Reception Site ____________________
- [ ] ...... Bridal Beauty:
    - [ ] ......Gown ____________________
    - [ ] ......Headpiece/Veil ____________________
    - [ ] ......Petticoat/Bustier ____________________
    - [ ] ......Jewelry ____________________
    - [ ] ......Shoes ____________________
    - [ ] [ ] .Going-away outfit (his and hers) ____________________
    - [ ] [ ] .Hair stylist, make-up ____________________
- [ ] ...... Tuxedo and Accessories ____________________
- [ ] ...... Honeymoon ____________________

Groom's Priorities

Think about what **really** matters to you and number this list accordingly. It should help you figure out the budget and where other people can "help."

- ☐ ..... Ceremony Site ____________
  - ☐ ...... Unity Candle ____________
  - ☐ ...... Huppot, Kiddush Cup ____________
- ☐ ..... Musician(s):
  - ☐ ...... Soloist ____________
  - ☐ ...... Ceremony Musician(s) ____________
  - ☐ ...... Reception Band/DJ ____________
- ☐ ..... Photographer ____________
- ☐ ..... Videographer ____________
- ☐ ..... Bachelor Party ____________
- ☐ ..... Rehearsal Dinner ____________
- ☐ ..... Reception Site ____________
- ☐ ..... Food & Beverages:
  - ☐ ...... Appetizers ____________
  - ☐ ...... Entrees ____________
  - ☐☐ . Cake (Primary, Groom's) ____________
  - ☐ ...... Drinks/Bar ____________
- ☐ ..... Rental items (tables, chairs, etc.) ____________
- ☐ ..... Favors ____________

☐...... Guest Book ____________________

☐...... Bird seed/Bubbles ____________________

☐...... Invitations ____________________

- ☐......Calligraphy ____________________

☐...... Limousine ____________________

☐...... Flowers:

- ☐......Bridal Bouquet ____________________
- ☐......Attendants ____________________
- ☐......Parents/Special Guests ____________________
- ☐......Ceremony Site ____________________
- ☐......Reception Site ____________________

☐...... Bridal Beauty:

- ☐......Gown ____________________
- ☐......Headpiece/Veil ____________________
- ☐......Petticoat/Bustier ____________________
- ☐......Jewelry ____________________
- ☐......Shoes ____________________
- ☐☐ .Going-away outfits (his and hers) ____
- ☐......Hair stylist ____________________
- ☐......Make-up ____________________

☐...... Tuxedo and Accessories ____________________

☐...... Honeymoon ____________________

Who Pays for What

Traditionally, the bride's parents paid for the wedding, the grooms' for the honeymoon, and the couple received gifts. Today, who pays for what is as unique as you and your families.

- ☐ ..... Ceremony site ______________________
  - ☐☐ . Officiant, counseling donation _______
  - ☐ ...... Janitor and misc. fees ______________
- ☐ ..... Marriage license ____________________
  - ☐ ...... Blood tests ____________________
  - ☐ ...... Medical examination ______________
- ☐ ..... Reception site ______________________
- ☐ ..... Caterer ___________________________
- ☐ ..... Rented items (tables, chairs) ____________
- ☐ ..... Coordinator _________________________
- ☐ ..... Florist ___________________________
- ☐ ..... Photographer ______________________
- ☐ ..... Videographer ______________________
- ☐ ..... Organist/ceremony musician __________
- ☐ ..... Soloist ___________________________
- ☐ ..... DJ/band __________________________
- ☐ ..... Rehearsal dinner ____________________

____

☐...... Bridal lunch ______________________

☐...... Hotel rooms for bridal party ____________

☐...... Bridesmaid's gifts __________________

☐...... Groomsmen's gifts _________________

☐...... Yarmulkes, Kittel __________________

☐...... Huppot ___________________________

☐☐. Glasses - to break and for toasting ________

☐...... Kiddush cup ______________________

☐...... Ketubah _________________________

☐☐. Limousine and parking _______________

☐...... Bride's cake ______________________

☐...... Groom's cake ______________________

☐...... Favors ___________________________

☐...... Guest book ________________________

☐...... Birdseed/bubbles ___________________

☐...... Coat check ________________________

☐☐. Bar and bartender ___________________

☐...... Restroom attendant _________________

☐...... Police officer ______________________

☐☐. Wedding bands ______________________

____

☐ ..... Wedding gown ____________________

- ☐ ...... Alterations ____________________
- ☐ ...... Headpiece ____________________
- ☐ ...... Hoop/petticoat ____________________
- ☐ ...... Undergarments ____________________
- ☐ ...... Jewelry ____________________
- ☐ ...... Trousseau ____________________
- ☐ ...... Going away outfit ____________________
- ☐☐ . Clean and preserve wedding gown __

☐ ..... Beauty appointments:

- ☐ ...... Hair stylist ____________________
- ☐ ...... Make-up artist ____________________
- ☐ ...... Manicure/pedicure ____________________

☐ ..... Misc. small stuff ____________________

☐ ..... Tuxedo rental ____________________

☐ ..... Groom's accessories ____________________

☐☐. Invitations and announcements ____________

☐ ..... Calligraphy ____________________

☐ ..... Postage for invitations ____________________

☐ ..... Thank you notes and postage ____________

☐☐. Airfare to wedding ____________________

☐ ..... Hotel the night before the wedding ________

☐...... Wedding night hotel room ____________

☐...... Honeymoon ____________

- ☐......Airfare ____________
- ☐......Hotels ____________
- ☐......Car rental ____________
- ☐......Special event tickets ____________

Totals:

Bride's Parents: $____________

Bride: $ ____________

Groom's Parents: $ ____________

Groom: $____________

Payments Made

If there are two check blocks, the first is for the first payment, the second is for the final payment.

☐ ..... Reserve ceremony site ____________________

$......... ________________________________

☐ ..... Janitor's fee (ceremony site) _______________

$......... ________________________________

☐☐. Officiant's fee / counseling donation _______

$......... ________________________________

☐ ..... Organist/ceremony musician _____________

$......... ________________________________

☐ ..... Soloist __________________________________

$......... ________________________________

☐ ..... Limousine _____________________________

$......... ________________________________

☐☐. Wedding gown and alterations ____________

$......... ________________________________

$......... ________________________________

☐☐. Tuxedo rental ___________________________

$......... ________________________________

$......... ________________________________

☐ ..... Rehearsal dinner site ___________________

$........ ______________________________

☐☐. Reception site ______________________

$........ ______________________________

$........ ______________________________

☐☐. Band/DJ ___________________________

$........ ______________________________

$........ ______________________________

☐☐. Photographer_______________________

$........ ______________________________

$........ ______________________________

☐☐. Videographer_______________________

$........ ______________________________

$........ ______________________________

☐☐. Baker _____________________________

$........ ______________________________

$........ ______________________________

☐☐. Caterer ____________________________

$........ ______________________________

$........ ______________________________

☐☐. Rental company (chairs, tables, etc.) ________

$........ ______________________________

$........ ______________________________

To-Do Lists

Groom

☐ ..... Select attendants and ask them. I know one man who asked his friends two weeks before the wedding. You MUST do it earlier than that! _______

☐ ..... Select ushers and ask them. One per 50 guests; they can be groomsmen also. ____________

☐ ..... Select tux store and style. ________________

☐ ..... Free tux rental for groom with other rentals?

☐ ..... Men's shoes (rented? loafers? patent leather?)

☐ ..... Get tux measurements____________________

☐☐. Get groomsmen to send their measurements to the tux shop by___________________________

☐......Send in your own measurements ____

☐ ..... See doctor for check-up and blood test. _____

☐ ..... Prepare guest list.________________________

☐☐. Tell parents how many guests they may invite and make them stick to it or pay for extras. __

____

☐ ..... Plan rehearsal dinner with your parents.____

☐☐☐..Arrange transportation to ceremony, reception, and honeymoon. ____________________

☐☐. Buy wedding bands with fiancé. ___________

☐☐. Have wedding bands engraved. ___________

☐☐. Check marriage license requirements. Set time with fiancé to get it, then get and keep track of it. Some states waive the minimum wait if you live out of state and request one with a good excuse, like insufficient vacation to fly back early.____________

☐...... Buy a wedding gift for your fiancé.__________

☐☐. Order boutonnieres, pay for bride's bouquet.

☐...... Tell attendants wedding and rehearsal details. ______________________________

☐...... Buy thank you gifts for your attendants. ____

☐...... Make moving arrangements. _____________

☐ ..... Talk to your family about problems._________

☐...... Plan honeymoon and wedding night hotel. __

☐☐ .Update passport, get visas (his & hers)

☐ ......Buy traveler's checks.______________

☐ ......Locate ATMs for your honeymoon.___

☐...... Double-check honeymoon reservations, confirmation numbers.____________________

If your fiancé wants you to help select something (like invitations) but the selection overwhelms you, ask them to narrow down the selection to a manageable number - just be clear whether manageable means twelve or three. And write thank you notes.

Bride's Mother

☐ ..... Select your gown. Tell the groom's mother what color you will be wearing so she can coordinate ____________________

Groom's Mother

☐ ..... Find out what color the Bride's mother is wearing and buy a dress that coordinates with it___

Attendants

Attendants are expected to pay for the purchase or rental of their wedding day clothing.

You may include the adults in the receiving line, but that is optional.

After the Mother of the Bride is seated, all the Groomsmen and Junior Groomsmen move to the right front (as you face the front) of the ceremony site with the Groom. The Groom stands closest to the center with the Best Man to his right. The Groomsmen and then Junior Groomsmen stand to the right of the Best Man.

For the Processional, the Junior Bridesmaids go first, followed by the Bridesmaids. The Maid/Matron of Honor fixes the Bride's train and veil during this time. She goes after the Bridesmaids. The Ring Bearer may go right before the Flower Girl or walk down with her. The Flower Girl goes last. There is either a new piece of music or a change in tempo in the processional, then the Bride and her Father/Escort go down the aisle.

Your officiant will tell you exactly where to stand, but generally the Bride is closest to the center with the Maid/Matron of Honor to her left, then her Bridesmaids and Junior Bridesmaids. The exact location of the Ring Bearer and Flower Girl varies a great deal, particularly during the ceremony.

There is no rule about which Bridesmaid or

Groomsman stand closest to the couple. You could arrange them by height, gown color (if you let each select a flattering color), how long you've known them, or any other order you want. You can also try to match the heights of Groomsmen and Bridesmaids.

Maid/Matron of Honor:

- Help with pre-wedding jobs, particularly addressing invitations and running errands.
- Plan and hostess a Bridal Shower with the other bridesmaids at least two weeks before the wedding. Bridal Showers used to be surprises, but it is now often necessary to coordinate with the Bride.
- Record shower and wedding gifts (optional). A Bridesmaid or other friend may also do this.
- Arrange for a Bachelorette Party, if desired.
- Arrive early for pictures and to help the bride dress. Remind her to eat something and use the restroom before dressing. Guess who gets to help when she needs to go to the restroom in all her bridal finery....
- For double-ring ceremonies, hold the Groom's ring until the appropriate point in the ceremony.
- Arrange the bride's train and veil as needed and bustle her train before the reception.
- Hold the bride's flowers as needed.
- Sign the wedding certificate as a witness. If she is not at least 21, designate another attendant as a witness.
- Make a toast at the reception (optional).

Bridesmaids:

- Help Bride with pre-wedding jobs, including addressing invitations.
- Help arrange a Bridal Shower.
- Record shower and wedding gifts (optional).
- Arrive early for pictures.

Junior Bridesmaids:

- Usually age eight to sixteen
- Dress in a similar style to adult Bridesmaids.
- May attend pre-wedding parties and showers.

Flower Girls:

- Usually two to seven years old.
- May sprinkle flower petals for the Bride to walk on. She may also just carry a small bouquet and look cute.

Best Man:

- Help the Groom with pre-wedding jobs.
- Arrange the Bachelor Party (if any).
- Drive the Groom to the church prior to the ceremony.
- Hold the Bride's ring and Marriage Certificate until the appropriate point in the ceremony.

- Sign the wedding certificate as a witness. If he is not at least 21, designate another attendant as a witness.
- Pay the officiant and other vendors (chauffeur, reception site) after the wedding. The Groom should give him labeled envelopes with checks for everyone who needs paid no later than the rehearsal dinner.
- Make the first toast at the reception.
- Arrange for the newlywed's honeymoon departure.
- Return rental tuxes to the tux shop. Someone else may do this, especially if the Best Man is from out of town.

Groomsmen:

- Perform all Usher duties (below).
- Arrive at the wedding location early and help set up.
- Seat guests of honor last (Bride's and Groom's parents, grandparents), in the pews reserved for them. The first pew or two on each side is saved for immediate family. The Bride's side goes on the left side, facing the front. The Groom's family goes on the right.
- Escort Bridesmaids.
- Direct guests at the reception.

- Move gifts to a safe location after the wedding.

Ushers:

- Give bulletins/programs to guests as they arrive and seat them. In the past, the Bride's friends and families sat on one side and the Groom's on the other. Today, guests are usually seated on the side with more space when they arrive.
- If you have Ushers who are not Groomsmen, they can seat late-arriving guests and put the aisle runner down for the Bride. This lets the Groomsmen stay up front with the Groom the entire time.
- The Head Usher (or Best Man) escorts the Mother of the Bride to her pew. She is the last one to be seated and this officially starts the wedding processional.

Junior Groomsmen:

- Dress in a style similar to adult Groomsmen.
- Usually age eight to sixteen.

Ring Bearers:

- Carry a pillow with fake ring(s) on it. The Honor Attendants have the real ones so they aren't dropped and lost.
- Usually two to seven years old.
- Be cute.

Bridal Party

Both sets of parents are part of the bridal party.

- ☐ ..... Maid/Matron of Honor ______________
- ☐ ..... Bridesmaid #1 ______________
- ☐ ..... Bridesmaid #2 ______________
- ☐ ..... Bridesmaid #3 ______________
- ☐ ..... Bridesmaid #4 ______________
- ☐ ..... Bridesmaid #5 ______________
- ☐ ..... Jr. Bridesmaid #1 ______________
- ☐ ..... Jr. Bridesmaid #2 ______________
- ☐ ..... Flower girl #1 ______________
- ☐ ..... Flower girl #2 ______________
- ☐ ..... Best Man ______________
- ☐ ..... Groomsman #1 ______________
- ☐ ..... Groomsman #2 ______________
- ☐ ..... Groomsman #3 ______________
- ☐ ..... Groomsman #4 ______________
- ☐ ..... Groomsman #5 ______________
- ☐ ..... Usher #1 ______________
- ☐ ..... Usher #2 ______________
- ☐ ..... Usher #3 ______________

☐...... Jr. Groomsman #1 ____________________

☐...... Jr. Groomsman #2 ____________________

☐...... Ring bearer ____________________

☐...... Escort bride down the aisle. Traditionally, this is the father of the bride. ____________________

Additional Assistants

☐☐☐... Acolytes/altar boys________________

☐ ..... Reader(s) ________________

☐ ..... Bulletin/program/mass book distribution __

____

☐ ..... Birdseed/bubble distribution ________________

☐☐. Seating his mother (step mother)________________

☐☐. Seating her mother (step mother) ________________

☐ ..... Ring pillow arrangements (watch ring bearer) ________________

☐ ..... Remove unity candle, Kiddush cup, etc. from ceremony site ________________

☐ ..... Reception Host/Hostess ________________

☐ ..... Arrange placecards ________________

☐ ..... Set up gift table________________

☐ ..... Reception set-up (take over cake knife, etc.) _

____

☐ ..... Collect leftover favors ________________

☐ ..... Final walk-through of ceremony and reception sites to check for forgotten items (incl. dressing rooms) ________________

____

☐...... Take wedding gown to dry cleaners ________

☐...... Store wedding gifts until after honeymoon __

☐...... House-sitter ______________________________

☐...... Pet-sitter/kennel __________________________

☐...... Baby-sitter ________________________________

☐...... Send bridal bouquet for preservation _______

☐...... Pay:

- ☐......Officiant ___________________________
- ☐......Organist ___________________________
- ☐......Soloist _____________________________
- ☐......Reception site ______________________
- ☐......Band/DJ _____________________________

____

☐...... Return rented tuxes ________________________

☐...... Return other rentals (tables, etc.) __________

____

☐...... Move and store top cake layer ______________

☐...... Retrieve gift money and deposit in bank ____

☐...... Church secretary. Send a thank you note if he or she typed up or copied your bulletins. ________

____

Thank You Gifts

Are any of your attendants' really short of space in their home? Do any have children or pets who might damage delicate gifts? What hobbies or interests do they have? Keep those things in mind when selecting gifts.

- Bookends
- Movie - romance like "Sleepless in Seattle"?
- Book
- Gift Certificate
- Keychain or money clip
- Picture Frame
- Engraved item
- Really good make-up brushes
- Music
- Tickets to a concert/show
- Toys (Lego can be a BIG hit with adults)
- Jewelry (cufflinks for men; women's can coordinate with their bridesmaids' gowns)
- Something related to your wedding - for a wedding near the Amish, hex signs or quilted pillows; at Walt Disney World, try something with Mickey Mouse
- Potted plants

- Perfume/cologne
- Stationery
- Jewelry / music box
- Snowglobe
- Travel or shaving kit
- Computer or board game (especially for kids)
- Good pen set or fountain pen
- Framed photo of you with your attendant
- Gift basket of scented soaps, etc.
- Something from their favorite sports team
- Something from their college/university
- Spa visit / certificate
- Something related to their interests
- A toy from Sharper Image, Brookstone or a similar store (very different from Toy 'r' Us toys)
- Still stuck? Check out gadget stores like Herrington and Hammacher Schlemmer, museum shops like the Smithsonian and the New York Metropolitan Museum of Art, or hobby companies like Bits & Pieces (puzzles) and the Gourmet Chef.

____

____

Thank You Gifts

This is a REALLY long list. You probably won't buy gifts for this many people. They're just reminders.

☐☐. His parents ______________________

$......... ______________________

☐☐. Her parents ______________________

$......... ______________________

☐ ..... Maid of Honor ______________________

$......... ______________________

☐ ..... Bridesmaid #1______________________

$......... ______________________

☐ ..... Bridesmaid #2______________________

$......... ______________________

☐ ..... Bridesmaid #3______________________

$......... ______________________

☐ ..... Bridesmaid #4______________________

$......... ______________________

☐ ..... Bridesmaid #5______________________

$......... ______________________

☐ ..... Best Man ______________________

$......... ______________________

☐...... Groomsman #1 ______________________

$......... ______________________

☐...... Groomsman #2 ______________________

$......... ______________________

☐...... Groomsman #3 ______________________

$......... ______________________

☐...... Groomsman #4 ______________________

$......... ______________________

☐...... Groomsman #5 ______________________

$......... ______________________

☐...... Usher #1 ______________________

$......... ______________________

☐...... Usher #2 ______________________

$......... ______________________

☐...... Usher #3 ______________________

$......... ______________________

☐...... Jr. Bridesmaid #1 ______________________

$......... ______________________

☐...... Jr. Bridesmaid #2 ______________________

$......... ______________________

☐...... Flower girl #1 ______________________

$......... ______________________

☐ ..... Flower girl #2 ______________________________

$......... ______________________________

☐ ..... Jr. Groomsman #1 ______________________________

$......... ______________________________

☐ ..... Jr. Groomsman #2 ______________________________

$......... ______________________________

☐ ..... Ring bearer ______________________________

$......... ______________________________

☐ ..... Reader ______________________________

$......... ______________________________

☐ ..... Reception set-up (take over cake knife, etc.) _

$......... ______________________________

☐ ..... Reception Host/Hostess ______________________________

$......... ______________________________

☐ ..... House-sitter ______________________________

$......... ______________________________

☐ ..... Pet watcher ______________________________

$......... ______________________________

____

____

____

____

Wedding Party Information Packets

☐ ..... Date, time, and exact ceremony location; approximate arrival time and location for bridal party (usually when photos start for men, when the bride gets dressed for women); expected end time of the reception.

____

☐ ..... Date, time, exact location, and dress code for the rehearsal and rehearsal dinner ____________

☐ ..... Date, time, location of other parties ________

____

☐ ..... Directions:

- ☐ ...... Hotel ________________________
- ☐ ...... Ceremony site (incl. from hotel) _____
- ☐ ...... Rehearsal dinner __________________
- ☐ ...... Reception _______________________

☐ ..... Job description, tasks you want them to do. Best Man gives a short toast, groomsmen seat people, etc. ______________________________

____

☐ ..... Men only:

- ☐ ...... Tux shop address/email ____________
- ☐ ...... Send in tux measurements by _______
- ☐ ...... Deposit of $___, final payment of $___

(Are checks accepted for final payment?) ____

☐ ......Shoes (rent? black patent? specifics?) _

☐ ......Pick up tuxes by__________on ________

☐ ......Time/place to arrive for photos ______

☐ ......Time to start seating guests __________

☐ ......Who will return tuxes to tux shop? When do they get them? (At the reception? after party?) ______________________________

____

☐ ...... Women only:

☐ ......Dress store address/email____________

☐ ......Send in measurements by ___________

☐ ......Pick up dress by ___________________

☐ ......Complete alterations by______________

☐ ......Shoes (Dyed? Color? Height?) _______

☐ ......Stocking color ______________________

☐ ......Hair/headpiece style ________________

☐ ......Jewelry ____________________________

☐ ......Time/place to arrive before ceremony to help bride dress ____________________

☐ ...... Hotel location and phone number __________

☐ ...... Registries. You're <u>supposed</u> to tell them. ____

____

Wedding Party Information Packets Sent

☐ ..... Wedding coordinator ____________________

☐ ..... Officiant ____________________

☐ ..... Cantor ____________________

☐☐. His Parents ____________________

☐☐. Her Parents ____________________

☐ ..... Maid of Honor ____________________

☐ ..... Bridesmaid #1 ____________________

☐ ..... Bridesmaid #2 ____________________

☐ ..... Bridesmaid #3 ____________________

☐ ..... Bridesmaid #4 ____________________

☐ ..... Bridesmaid #5 ____________________

☐ ..... Jr. Bridesmaid #1 ____________________

☐ ..... Jr. Bridesmaid #2 ____________________

☐ ..... Flower girl #1 ____________________

☐ ..... Flower girl #2 ____________________

☐ ..... Best Man ____________________

☐ ..... Groomsman #1 ____________________

☐ ..... Groomsman #2 ____________________

☐ ..... Groomsman #3 ____________________

☐ ..... Groomsman #4 ____________________

☐...... Groomsman #5 ____________________

☐...... Usher #1 ____________________

☐...... Usher #2 ____________________

☐...... Usher #3 ____________________

☐...... Jr. Groomsman #1 ____________________

☐...... Jr. Groomsman #2 ____________________

☐...... Ring bearer ____________________

☐...... Acolytes/altar boys ____________________

____

☐...... Reader ____________________

☐...... Reception Host/Hostess ____________________

☐...... Reception set-up (take over cake knife, etc.)__

____

☐...... Organist. The soloist and organist normally meet on their own and only the organist attends the rehearsal. The organist may charge a fee to attend; it is worth it. If the soloist attends, send them a packet.____________________

____

☐...... Other ____________________

____

____

Ceremony and Reception

The marriage ceremony is when you actually become husband and wife. The reception and everything else is a celebration of the marriage ceremony. If you read enough bridal books, you may forget that anything happens between getting dressed and the post-ceremony photo shoot. Your officiant is the best guide for your ceremony.

If you are getting married in a house of worship (church, synagogue, etc.), your wedding is automatically a *private religious service*. Because it is a religious service, there are usually restrictions on photography, videography, music and other areas your officiant will advise you of. These can be frustrating, but your officiant is not trying to be difficult. They are following their beliefs. Everyone must follow the same restrictions. For example, some pastors only officiate inside a church. Outside "in God's Creation" is not the same to them.

Of course, it's often easier to find a church or synagogue to be married in and to get the time you want than to find a secular site, and much easier than a reception site. Discuss requirements and restrictions with your officiant early in the planning process. Areas to talk about include counseling requirements; if you must both be baptized; and restrictions on: photography (flash allowed?), videography (stationary or moving?), music (only one secular piece, or more?), flowers (must you leave them for Sabbath services?), birdseed or bubbles, and the receiving line location.

Protestant ceremonies often provide bulletins (programs) explaining who is in the bridal party and giving special notes from the couple. Even if you don't use a bulletin or program, this is a handy list of important details.

If you are getting married or having your reception outside, buy nice sunglasses. You'll probably be wearing them in a lot of your pictures.

If you have more than about 100 guests, you should seriously consider having a receiving line. You probably won't have another chance to talk to some of your guests. Also, I hate to say this, but you may never see some of them again. Just keep the line to your parents and the two of you.

Financially, having an open bar (you pay for everything) or a cash bar (guests pay) is a major consideration. It is possible to compromise on this by providing a few drinks (a keg of beer, champagne punch, margaritas, soda) and having a cash bar for all other alcohol. You can also limit how long drinks are served.[3]

If you have specific dietary restrictions, including kosher needs or allergies, be very clear about this

---

[3] Lawsuits are also a consideration. Limiting how long drinks are served means that there is more time between when guests drink and when they leave.

with the caterer. You should seriously consider having one vegetarian entrée (like pasta primavera) because there are so many vegetarians today.

Regarding your wedding cake: get your favorite flavor. The only questionable choice today is actually white. No one will be offended, but it doesn't rise nicely. You can even get a chocolate croquembouche - a chocolate covered craft base with pieces of chocolate stuck on with toothpicks. The major advantage to a yellow (or white) cake with white frosting is that it won't leave a big mark if you drop it on your gown.

We alternated layers of strawberry and yellow cake. We also had an ice cream sundae bar for dessert. Everyone loved them both. Also, if you don't want to freeze your top layer for a year, you could freeze it until your one-month anniversary or a similar date. We ate ours after our honeymoon, while we opened our gifts.

Hints and Tips

- Take your engagement ring off (or put it on another finger) before the actual wedding ceremony. Ask your Maid of Honor to remind you.
- Traditionally, the bride's friends and family sat on one side and the groom's on the other. Today, guests often sit on the side with more space when they arrive.

Ceremony site and officiant questions:

- What are the requirements - including counseling? How much is the usual donation for counseling?
- Are aisle runners, musical instruments, Huppot, or unity candleholders provided? What decorations are provided?
- Is tossing rice allowed? Many sites no longer allow rice to be tossed and couples need to use birdseed or bubbles instead.
- What are the restrictions on music?
- What restrictions are there for photographers and videographers?
- Are you expected to leave any of the flowers for Sabbath services?
- When can you access the site to decorate it? To prepare on your wedding day?

- Are there other weddings that day?
- Can you have a receiving line? Where?
- Cost for the ceremony? Janitorial service?
- Does your officiant want your marriage license at the rehearsal? If he takes it a day early, it's one less worry on your wedding day.
- Is there an electric stained glass window in the front of the church? If there is, it may be turned off at the same time as the candles. Have your acolyte (or officiant) turn it back on before any pictures are taken.

Reception site questions:

- Is there a discounted price or different menu for kids?
- How much do carafes of wine cost vs. bottles? Carafes are often cheaper.

About your reception:

- Many couples skip the bouquet and garter toss. Children enjoy trying to catch them. You can buy cheap ($2 or so) toss garters at craft stores.
- White cake doesn't rise nicely. Yellow is a better choice. So are chocolate and carrot.
- If your wedding is large, supplement your fancy wedding cake with a simple sheet cake that's cut in the kitchen.

- Buy some games for small children to play with at the reception. A piñata. Crayons and a coloring book. Inflatable musical instruments. Anything to entertain them after dinner is over.

- We typed up a one page "story" of our life together - how we met, places we liked to go on dates, how and where he proposed, meeting each other's families and our honeymoon plans. We copied them onto bond paper, rolled them up and gave one to each guest. It was a conversation starter and answered many common questions so we weren't telling the same few stories over and over. This gave us more time to talk to friends.

- If you write your story, roll the paper around a dowel rod. Use the inexpensive silver or gold "rings" sold in craft stores and bridal catalogs to hold them.

Bridal Beauty

☐ ..... Gown:

- ☐ ...... First alterations/dry clean 4 weeks before formal portrait, <u>at least</u> 3 months before the wedding ____________
- ☐ ...... Final fitting ____________
- ☐ ...... Picked up ____________
- ☐ ...... Pressed and hung up ____________

☐ ..... Petticoat/hoop ____________

☐ ..... Undergarments ____________

☐☐. Stockings, a spare pair, garter belt ____________

☐☐. Headpiece and veil ____________

☐ ..... Gloves ____________

☐☐. Garters (one to keep, one to toss) ____________

☐ ..... Shoes ____________

☐ ..... Jacket/coat/cape ____________

☐ ..... Bridal bag:

- ☐☐. Safety pins, bobbie pins ____________
- ☐☐. Needle and thread ____________
- ☐ ...... Spare stockings ____________
- ☐ ...... Clear nail polish ____________
- ☐ ...... Handkerchief ____________
- ☐ ...... Contact lens/eye drops ____________

☐ ......Contact lens case ____________________

☐ ......Hard candy/cough drops ____________

☐ ......Sunscreen, sunglasses ______________

☐ ......Advil/Tylenol ______________________

☐ ......Antihistamines ____________________

☐ ......Spare earring backs ________________

☐ ......Small pad of paper and pen _________

☐ ......Extra camera memory _______________

☐☐☐.Necklace, earrings, bracelet ______________

☐...... Sunglasses, check how they look with gown _

☐☐. Haircut (trial, and final appointment) _______

____

☐☐. Make-up application (trial, final appointment) ___________________________________

____

☐☐. Manicure and pedicure _________________

☐...... Going away outfit (with shoes and accessories) ___________________________________

____

Thigh highs have solid strips of rubber at the top hold them up, not garters. It's easier to use the ladies room than with full nylons or gartered stockings. Try them before the wedding if you're interested but unsure. Good ones stay up for hours, even with dancing.

Bulletin/Program

- ☐ ..... Music (see separate sheet)________________
- ☐ ..... Participants (including their relationship):
  - ☐ ...... Officiant ________________
  - ☐ ...... Cantor ________________
  - ☐ ...... Maid of Honor ________________
  - ☐ ...... Bridesmaid #1 ________________
  - ☐ ...... Bridesmaid #2 ________________
  - ☐ ...... Bridesmaid #3 ________________
  - ☐ ...... Bridesmaid #4 ________________
  - ☐ ...... Bridesmaid #5 ________________
  - ☐ ...... Jr. Bridesmaid #1 ________________
  - ☐ ...... Jr. Bridesmaid #2 ________________
  - ☐ ...... Flower girl #1 ________________
  - ☐ ...... Flower girl #2 ________________
  - ☐ ...... Best Man ________________
  - ☐ ...... Groomsman #1 ________________
  - ☐ ...... Groomsman #2 ________________
  - ☐ ...... Groomsman #3 ________________
  - ☐ ...... Groomsman #4 ________________
  - ☐ ...... Groomsman #5 ________________
  - ☐ ...... Usher #1 ________________
  - ☐ ...... Usher #2 ________________

☐ ......Usher #3 ____________________________

☐ ......Jr. Groomsman #1____________________

☐ ......Jr. Groomsman #2____________________

☐ ......Ring bearer___________________________

☐ ......Organist/ceremony musician________

☐ ......Soloist ______________________________

☐ ......Acolytes/altar boys _________________

☐ ......Reader_______________________________

☐ ......Bulletin/mass book distribution _____

☐ ......Birdseed/bubble distribution________

☐☐ .His/her grandparents _______________

☐☐ .His/her godparents _________________

☐☐ . Readings:

____

____

☐...... Special notes (e.g., bride's gown is an heirloom):

____

____

Christian bookstores sell blank bulletins. They cost *a lot* less than programs by invitation companies. Send thank you notes if someone types and copies them for you.

Music

Ceremony

☐ ..... OK selections with your ceremony site (churches often limit secular pieces) **and musician** - Do they know it? Can they learn it (for a price)? ___

☐ ..... Organist/other ________________

☐ ...... Fee $ ________________

☐ ..... Soloist ________________

☐ ...... Fee $ ________________

☐ ..... Other musician ________________

☐ ...... Fee $ ________________

☐ ..... Pre-ceremony (about 20 minutes). Many popular pre-ceremony pieces are only 2-3 minutes, so you'll need about six.

____

____

____

____

____

☐ ..... Solos (usually 2-3) ________________

____

____

- ☐ Unity Candle Solo ____________________

☐...... Processional ____________________

☐...... Hymn ____________________

☐...... Communion ____________________

☐...... Recessional ____________________

____

Reception

☐...... Name of DJ/band ____________________

- ☐ ......Fee $ ____________________

☐...... DJ/band start time__________; end time _____

☐...... First dance ____________________

☐...... Father/daughter dance ____________________

☐...... Mother/son dance (or one parents' dance) __

☐...... Garter toss (optional) ____________________

☐...... Bouquet toss (optional) ____________________

☐...... Start of money dance (optional) ____________

☐...... Last dance ____________________

____

____

In addition to bridal magazine and online lists of wedding music, some music stores (the kind that sell musicians sheet music) sell CDs full of them.

Musical Options

Ceremony

Pre-Ceremony

"So This Is Love" (Cinderella) - David, Hoffman, Livingston
"Ave Maria" - Schubert
"Jesu, Joy of Man's Desiring" - Bach
"Let Us Ever Walk With Jesus" - Gieschen
"Processional in 'C' " - Hopson
"Wedding Bells" - Peale

Processionals - can also be Pre-Ceremony Music

"Bridal Chorus" ("Lohengrin") - Wagner
"Canon in D" - Pachelbel
"Dance of the Sugar Plum Fairies" - Tchaikovsky
"Ode to Joy" - Beethoven
"Rondeau" ("Masterpiece Theater" theme) - Mouret
"Trumpet Tune" - Purcell
"Trumpet Voluntary" - Dupuis
"Trumpet Voluntary in 'D Major' " - Clarke
"Waltz of the Flowers" - Tchaikovsky
"Where'er You Walk (Semele)" - Handel

Solos - these can also be used for the Reception

"All I Ask of You" - Norbet and Callahan
"The Bride's Prayer" - Good
"God, a Woman and a Man" - Peele
"The Irish Wedding Song" - traditional
"The Lord's Prayer" - Malotte
"Now Thank We All Our God" - Bach
"Savior Like A Shepherd Lead Us" - Bradbury
"Simple Gifts" - Shaker Song
"Song of Ruth" - Eilers
"The Unity Candle Song" - Sullivan
"The Wedding Prayer" - Dunlap

"The Wedding Song" - Paul Stookey"

Recessionals - can also be Pre-Ceremony Music

"All Creatures of Our God and King" - Williams
"Alla Hornpipe" from "Water Music" - Handel
"The Arrival of the Queen of Sheba" - Handel
"Cantata No. 51 - Alleluia" - Bach
"Pomp and Circumstance" - Elgar
"Rondeau" ("Masterpiece Theater" theme) - Mouret
"Russian Dance" - Tchaikovsky
"Toccata Symphony V" - Widor
"Trumpet Tune" - Stanley
"Wedding March" ("Midsummer Night's Dream") - Mendelssohn

Reception

"All I Ask of You" - Michael Crawford
"As Time Goes By" - Irving Berlin
"Because You Loved Me" - Celine Dion
"Butterfly Kisses" - Bob Carlisle
"Daddy's Little Girl" - Burke and Gerlach
"Endless Love" - Diana Ross and Lionel Richie.
"Hopelessly Devoted to You" - Olivia Newton John
"I Swear" - J.M. Montgomery - All 4 One
"I Will Always Love You" - Whitney Houston
"Just the Way You Are" - Billy Joel
Frank Sinatra - anything he did
"Sunrise, Sunset" - from "Fiddler on the Roof"
"Time in a Bottle" - Jim Croce
"Unchained Melody" - Righteous Brothers
"Unforgettable" - Natalie Cole or Nat King Cole
"Up Where We Belong" - Joe Cocker, Jennifer Warnes
"Woman" - John Lennon
"Wonderful Tonight" - Eric Clapton
"You are the Sunshine of My Life" - Stevie Wonder
"We've Only Just Begun" - The Carpenters

Reception

Estimate #1

☐ ..... Company Name ____________________________

☐ ..... Address ____________________________

☐ ..... Phone number (_____)____________________

☐ ..... Website ____________________________

☐ ..... Deposit of $____If cancelled, is it returned?__

☐ ..... In-house caterer?____Must you use them? __

☐ ..... Per person costs:

- ☐ ...... Meals cost from $_______ to $ _______
- ☐ ...... Drinks cost from $______ to $ _______

☐ ..... Is there a wine corkage fee? $______________

☐ ..... Can you bring in your own cake? __________

Is there a cutting/serving fee? ___________________

☐ ..... Minimum _____ and maximum number ____

☐ ..... Number per table____ Dance floor size _____

☐ ..... Times and dates available_________________

Charges if you run overtime $ ___________________

When can you set-up/decorate site?______________

Other events at the site that day?_______________

☐ ..... Decorations available ____________________

☐ ..... Is there a coatroom? $______Bartender? $ ___

Doorman? $_______ Ample parking? $ __________

Police/security? $_______ Other charges $ _______

☐...... When is a final count required? __________

____

____

____

____

Estimate #2

☐...... Company Name ____________________

☐...... Address __________________________

☐...... Phone number (_____) ________________

☐...... Website ___________________________

☐...... Deposit of $____ If cancelled, is it returned? __

☐...... In-house caterer? ____ Must you use them? ___

☐...... Per person costs:

- ☐ ......Meals cost from $_______ to $_______
- ☐ ......Drinks cost from $______ to $_______

☐...... Is there a wine corkage fee? $ ___________

☐...... Can you bring in your own cake? ________

Is there a cutting/serving fee? _______________

☐...... Minimum _____ and maximum number ____

☐ ..... Number per table____ Dance floor size _____

☐ ..... Times and dates available__________________

Charges if you run overtime $ ____________________

When can you set-up/decorate site?______________

Other events at the site that day?_________________

☐ ..... Decorations available _____________________

☐ ..... Is there a coatroom? $______Bartender? $ ___

Doorman? $_______Ample parking? $____________

Police/security? $________Other charges $________

☐ ..... When is a final count required?____________

____

____

____

____

Estimate #3

☐ ..... Company Name __________________________

☐ ..... Address _________________________________

☐ ..... Phone number (_____)____________________

☐ ..... Website _________________________________

☐ ..... Deposit of $____If cancelled, is it returned?__

☐ ..... In-house caterer?____Must you use them? __

☐...... Per person costs:

☐ ......Meals cost from $_______ to $________

☐ ......Drinks cost from $______ to $________

☐...... Is there a wine corkage fee? $ ______________

☐...... Can you bring in your own cake? __________

Is there a cutting/serving fee? ____________________

☐...... Minimum _____ and maximum number ____

☐...... Number per table____ Dance floor size _____

☐...... Times and dates available _______________

Charges if you run overtime $ ___________________

When can you set-up/decorate site? ______________

Other events at the site that day? _________________

☐...... Decorations available ____________________

☐...... Is there a coatroom? $______Bartender? $ ___

Doorman? $_______Ample parking? $ ____________

Police/security? $________Other charges $ ________

☐...... When is a final count required? ____________

____

____

____

____

Menu/Reception Arrangements

Final count due on___Adults___Kids___Babies___

Meal #1_______ Meal #2________Meal #3________

Some reception sites charge less for children 4-11 years old, and even less for kids under 4, or offer a kids menu.

☐ ..... Hors d'oeuvres (during photo shoot) _______

____

☐ ..... Appetizers (served with the meal) _________

____

☐ ..... Salad and dressing________________________

☐ ..... Entree #1 (Vegetarian)____________________

____

☐ ..... Entree #2 _______________________________

____

☐ ..... Entree #3 _______________________________

____

☐ ..... Dessert __________________________________

____

☐ ..... Kosher food - milchig (dairy) _____________

flayshig (meat) ___________________________

☐...... Cake flavor ____________________

☐...... Punch flavor ____________________

☐...... Bar (does site permit drinking? open? cash?) _

____

☐...... Drink for toasting ____________________

☐...... Hours reception site is reserved for ________

____

☐...... Person(s) who will decorate site ____________

☐...... When can reception site be decorated? ______

____

☐...... Decorations ____________________

____

☐...... Will smoking be permitted? ______________

☐...... Wedding day contact for the reception site; give this name to the site. This person will handle problems so you and your spouse can enjoy your reception. ____________________

____

☐...... Person to bring drinks to bridal party during the photo shoot. ____________________

☐...... Restrictions to note ____________________

____

Reception Decorations, etc.

☐ ..... Toasting glasses ____________________

☐ ..... Attendants' toasting glasses ____________

☐ ..... Bouquet holder to clamp onto table ______

____

☐ ..... Cake knife set ____________________

☐ ..... Cake boxes ______________________

☐ ..... Favors___________________________

____

☐ ..... Napkins _________________________

☐ ..... Matchbooks_______________________

☐ ..... Thank you scrolls___________________

____

☐ ..... Basket or wishing well for cards. Have it watched so nothing is lost; some will have money inside. ______________________________

____

☐ ..... Table centerpieces. They don't need to be elaborate. You can have something simple like a single rose, baby's breath and a few non-Mylar balloons.______________________________

____

☐...... Photos of you and your fiancé. It's affordable, a conversation starter for your guests, and your friends and family will probably enjoy looking at photos of you two having fun. ____________________

____

____

☐...... Place cards ______________________________

☐...... Napkins rings ____________________________

☐...... After-dinner entertainment to keep kids occupied so grown-ups can visit longer – ad libs, dominos, maybe even a baby-sitter. ____________

____

____

☐...... Balloons _________________________________

☐...... Arch ____________________________________

☐...... Potted trees, plants ________________________

☐...... Fountain _________________________________

☐...... Lighted marquee ___________________________

☐...... Ice sculptures ____________________________

☐...... Candles __________________________________

____

____

Reception Program

Before your wedding day, give a copy of this to your MC and a second copy to the person handling last-minute problems on your wedding day.

☐ ..... Reception starts ______________________________

____

☐ ..... Serve bridal party drinks during the photo shoot. ______________________________

____

☐ ..... Bride and groom arrive______________________

____

☐ ..... Introductions ______________________________

____

☐ ..... Receiving line ______________________________

____

☐ ..... Dinner served ______________________________

____

☐ ..... Blessing(s) ______________________________

____

☐ ..... Toast(s)______________________________

____

☐...... First dance ____________________

☐...... Father/daughter dance ____________________

☐...... Mother/son dance ____________________

☐...... Cake cutting ____________________

☐...... Bouquet toss ____________________

☐...... Garter toss ____________________

☐...... Money dance ____________________

☐...... Last dance ____________________

☐...... Bride and groom leave ____________________

Rehearsal and Rehearsal Dinner

Rehearsal

☐ ..... Location ______________________________

☐ ..... Directions to location ____________________

____

____

☐ ..... Time: from __________ until __________

☐ ..... Payments for:

- ☐ ...... Ceremony site ____________________
- ☐ ...... Officiant _________________________
- ☐ ...... Organist/other musician __________

☐ ..... "Bouquet" of ribbons from bridal shower ___

Ask ceremony site if you can leave the following after the rehearsal. If not, choose a friend to take care of them. This leaves less to worry about on your wedding day.

☐ ..... Bubbles/birdseed ______________________

☐ ..... Bulletins/programs ____________________

☐ ..... Guest book and pen ____________________

☐ ..... Unity candles (one pillar, two tapers), holder

☐☐. Marriage license, Ketubah (check with your officiant – some take them early so you can't forget)

☐ ..... Huppot and poles ______________________

☐...... Kiddush cup, glasses ______________________

☐...... Ring bearer's pillow ______________________

☐...... Flower girl's basket ______________________

☐...... Basket for birdseed ______________________

____

____

Rehearsal Dinner

☐...... Location ______________________

☐...... Directions to location ______________________

____

☐...... Time: from ____________ until ____________

☐...... Non-bridal party guests ______________________

____

____

☐...... Menu ______________________

____

____

____

☐...... Distribute Thank-You Gifts ______________________

____

Religious Ceremony

If you are married in a house of worship, your wedding is a religious service and you must follow certain guidelines, including limits on photography and secular music. Talk to your officiant to learn these rules.

☐ ..... Church/temple ("site") reserved__________

- ☐ ...... Address:__________
- ☐ ...... Phone number __________

____

☐ ..... Counseling with officiant __________

☐ ..... Fees related to site use:

- ☐ ...... Officiant performing ceremony ______
- ☐ ...... Counseling by officiant __________
- ☐ ...... Site use __________
- ☐ ...... Janitorial service __________
- ☐ ...... Other __________

☐ ..... Site requirements/restrictions:

- ☐ ...... Music __________
- ☐ ...... Photography/videography __________
- ☐ ...... Flowers (where should they be delivered? are altar flowers to be left at the site?) __________
- ☐ ...... Bubbles/birdseed__________

- ☐ ......Other restrictions ____________________

☐...... Readings selected - approved by officiant:

- ☐ ......Reading #1 ____________________
- ☐ ......Reading #2 ____________________
- ☐ ......If Biblical, version of the Bible. (King James uses thees and thous; Revised Standard – RSV – doesn't). Ask your officiant which is used. If you have a strong preference, provide your own Bible. ________

☐...... Room for Bride/Groom to dress in ________

☐...... Rehearsal time ____________________

☐...... Sufficient reserved parking ____________

☐...... Is proof of baptism required? ___________

☐...... Color of the day (so you don't clash horribly)

☐...... Homily (a mini-sermon) ____________

☐...... Kneeler ____________________

☐☐. Crowns ____________________

☐☐. Kiddush cup, cup for wine ____________

☐☐. Glasses to break w/napkin or pouch _______

☐...... Huppot and poles ____________________

☐...... Yarmulkes ____________________

☐...... Kittel for groom ____________________

☐☐. Ketubah, correct color pen ____________

· Remarriage

☐ ..... Things he wants to do, or skip. ____________

____

☐ ..... Things she wants to do, or skip. ___________

____

☐ ..... Is this a first wedding for one of you? ______

____

☐ ..... Things you DO need/want to register for. __

____

☐ ..... Things you DON'T need/want to register for

____

☐ ..... His expectations for the wedding.__________

____

☐ ..... Her expectations for the wedding. _________

____

☐ ..... His expectations for the marriage.__________

____

☐ ..... Her expectations for the marriage. _________

____

____

Involving Your Children

Some of these are for small children, others are for adult children.

☐ ..... Part of the unity candle ceremony. __________

____

☐ ..... Part of the wedding party. ________________

____

☐ ..... Invited to all showers, pre-wedding parties.

____

☐ ..... Submitted their guest list with a few friends.

____

☐ ..... Selected/approved their wedding outfit.____

____

☐ ..... Have their own camera. ___________________

____

☐ ..... Included in ceremony.____________________

____

☐ ..... Special gift for them. ___________________

____

____

☐...... Read a special selection.________________

____

☐...... Have them make a drawing representing your wedding. Have it matted and have your guests sign the mat instead of a guest book. ______

____

☐...... About two weeks before your wedding, go out somewhere they really want to go and do something not related to the wedding. Don't bring your fiancé unless <u>your child</u> asks you to. ________

____

☐...... Listen to <u>their</u> concerns about <u>their</u> new step-parent and other family changes ______________

____

____

____

____

____

____

____

____

Honeymoon

Your honeymoon is an important part of your wedding. Have fun with it! If you plan your honeymoon yourself, it will be more work than using a travel agent, but you will have more control over the cost and can go exactly where you want to. Of course, experienced travel agents can help you find hidden jewels you might miss.

The first and most important step is to decide where you want to go. There are two pages for each of you to write the kinds of places you would go and things you would do on your ideal vacation. Often, the first place that comes to mind for a honeymoon is a nice, sunny island but that isn't everyone's ideal vacation. If you want to go kayaking or visit Bucharest, go for it!

Check the amenities at your hotel before packing. To my surprise, we needed bathing suits in October in England because the timeshare had an indoor pool and sauna. We also needed waterproof shoes and raincoats because it was still England.

No matter what you do, make sure you have plenty of time to rest so you aren't too tired for romantic evenings. Remember, it's your honeymoon! You'll take a lot more vacations together, so you can go back if you miss a few fun activities.

Hints and Tips

- If you buy lingerie a few months in advance, you can put it in a drawer or suitcase with a sachet. By your honeymoon, it should smell GREAT! If you do, then put a sheet of plastic wrap under the sachet--occasionally, oil from spices can leak and stain your things.
- If you go to a beach and one of you is fair, be very careful to always wear enough waterproof sunscreen, and be sure to reapply often. More than one person has had their honeymoon ruined by a bad sunburn.
- When making reservations, use the bride's maiden name because she won't have proof of her name change (if any) yet.
- Most credit cards have a pin number. You may need it to use your card outside of the USA.
- Search sites like Travelocity.com and PriceLine.com for the lowest possible airfare. Southwest.com is the exclusive online distributor for Southwest Airlines tickets.
- Hotels consider anything after 6 pm to be a late arrival. If you will arrive at your wedding night or honeymoon hotel(s) later than 6 pm, be sure to have your room(s) guaranteed for late arrival.
- You can locate nearby ATMs before leaving on your honeymoon by asking your bank for a listing or by searching online.

Car Rental

Domestic and International:

☐ ..... Alamo 888-233-8749 Alamo.com ______

☐ ..... Avis 800- 633-3469 Avis.com________

☐ ..... Budget 800-218-7992 Budget.com______

☐ ..... Dollar 800-800-4000 Dollar.com ______

☐ ..... Enterprise 800-261-7331 Enterprise.com___

☐ ..... Hertz 800-654-3131 Hertz.com_______

☐ ..... National 800-501-9010 NationalCar.com_

☐ ..... Thrifty 800-847-4389 Thrifty.com______

Questions to ask:

☐ ..... If one of you is under 25, is there a surcharge? ____________________________________

☐ ..... Is the car stick or automatic? It's worth paying for automatic in left-side drive countries, and may not be a choice. _______________________

☐ ..... Is the trunk covered? (esp. outside US) _____

☐ ..... Is there an additional charge for your spouse to drive too? There usually isn't in the US, but may be in other countries. ___________________________

☐ ..... Where is the car pick up / drop off?________

____

☐ ..... How long does it take to get from the car

drop-off point to the airport terminals and vice versa? ____________________

☐...... If you arrive and depart from different places, is there a drop-off location closer to your destination? ____________________

____

☐...... Is there a courtesy shuttle to your hotel? ____

☐...... Discounts available/used (AAA, your employer, airline tie-ins) ____________________

____

☐...... If you don't use a credit card, is a refundable cash deposit required? ($1,000+ isn't unusual) _____

☐...... What is the minimum deposit taken from a credit card? You may end up close to your limit. ___

☐...... Cost $______for rental from _____until______

☐ ......Cost with unlimited mileage is $ _____

☐ ......______ miles free, $____ per extra mile

☐...... Size car reserved ____________________

☐...... Amenities requested (convertible?) _________

____

☐☐. Make and model of car reserved. ___________

☐...... Cost/gallon if you don't top off the gas tank

____

Potential Destinations

Good information sources include tourist boards, travel agents, travel books, and the Internet.

Type of Trip:

☐ ..... Cultural trip (another country, museums)____

☐ ..... Adventure (kayaking, skiing) ______________

☐ ..... Educational (snorkeling, glass blowing) ____

☐ ..... Relaxation (the beach, a spa) ______________

☐ ..... Cruise________________________________

Accommodations:

☐ ..... Bed and Breakfast ________________________

☐ ..... Hotel/motel ____________________________

☐ ..... 4 Star hotel_____________________________

☐ ..... All inclusive resort________________________

☐ ..... House or bungalow _______________________

Locale:

☐ ..... Mountains ______________________________

☐ ..... Desert__________________________________

☐ ..... Beach __________________________________

☐ ..... City_____________________________________

☐ ..... Country _________________________________

____

Restrictions:

☐...... Budget $ ____________________________

☐...... Start on ______________, end on __________

☐...... Minimum of ____days, maximum of ___days

☐...... No travel via (boat, plane, etc.) __________

(due to motion sickness, phobias, etc.) __________

☐...... Be within ______hours, ______miles of _____

☐...... Speak these languages (international) _______

☐...... Activities must include ________________

____

____

Potential Destinations:

☐...... Regions/countries ____________________

____

☐...... Cities ________________________________

____

____

☐...... Resorts _____________________________

____

____

His Dream Vacation

If you could go anywhere, do anything on vacation, what would it be? Maybe climbing Mt. Everest is out of the question but mountain climbing lessons (or very long hikes) aren't. If you want to try French cooking but can't afford Europe, maybe Cajun cooking in New Orleans is for you. The idea is for to write down places you dream of going, then figure out what you would both enjoy and can realistically do. This is the place for wild ideas! Dream big!

Cities (domestic and international): ______________

____

____

Countries: ____________________________________

____

____

Historical sites (Tower of London, Hollywood & Vine): ____

____

____

Natural wonders (Mt. Everest, Grand Canyon): ____

____

____

Cultural sights (the Louvre, NFL Hall of Fame): ____

____

____

____

Sports to try (rollerblading, mountain climbing): ___

____

____

____

____

Skills to learn (cooking, race car driving):__________

____

____

____

Important vacation activities (sunbathing,):________

____

____

____

Restrictions (motion sickness, medical, phobias)____

____

Her Dream Vacation

If you could go anywhere, do anything on vacation, what would it be? Maybe climbing Mt. Everest is out of the question but mountain climbing lessons (or very long hikes) aren't. If you want to try French cooking but can't afford Europe, maybe Cajun cooking in New Orleans is for you. The idea is for to write down places you dream of going, then figure out what you would both enjoy and can realistically do. This is the place for wild ideas! Dream big!

Cities (domestic and international): ______________

____

____

Countries: ____________________________________

____

____

Historical sites (Versailles, the Alamo): ___________

____

____

Natural wonders (Mt. Everest, Grand Canyon): ____

____

____

____

Cultural sights (Grand Ole Opry, the Met in NYC): _

____

____

____

Sports to try (scuba diving, skiing): ______________

____

____

____

____

Skills to learn (massage, trapeze artist): ___________

____

____

____

Important vacation activities (sunbathing,):________

____

____

____

Restrictions (motion sickness, medical, phobias)____

____

Final Plans

☐ ..... Destination ______________________

☐ ..... Travel agent ______________________

☐ ..... Airline and confirmation number __________

____

☐ ..... Arrival date and time ________________

____

☐ ..... Departure date and time________________

____

☐ ..... Rental car company and confirmation number______________________________

____

☐ ..... Wedding night hotel ________________

- ☐ ...... Phone number ________________
- ☐ ...... Website ____________________
- ☐ ...... Address ____________________
- ☐ ...... Confirmation number ____________

☐ ..... Honeymoon hotel(s) ________________

- ☐ ...... Phone number ________________
- ☐ ...... Website ____________________
- ☐ ...... Address ____________________
- ☐ ...... Confirmation number ____________

☐☐. Contact information given to:

- ☐☐ .Family ______________________
- ☐☐ .Assistants ______________________
- ☐ ......Baby-sitter ______________________

☐...... Check if insurance is valid (esp. overseas):

- ☐ ......Rental car. Read your credit card's fine print. You may be covered in the USA but not other countries. If you're insured in the USA, using that saves you money. If you go outside the USA, take the name and operator number of the person who confirmed coverage so you aren't charged VAT tax. ____
- ☐ ......Floater policy for ring(s) valid ________
- ☐ ......Health ______________________

☐...... Special cell phone use instructions (especially internationally)______________________

☐☐. Vacation request submitted to employers ___

☐...... Registered for honeymoon (as a gift) at _____

____

☐...... Local maps ______________________________

____

When you make reservations, you may need to use the bride's maiden name because she won't have proof of her name change (if any) yet.

Budget

- ☐ ..... Destination ______________________
- ☐ ..... From ____________ until ____________
- ☐ ..... Airfare per person ________________
- ☐ ..... Car rental w/mileage charges __________
- ☐ ..... Gasoline ________________________
- ☐ ..... Airport shuttles ___________________
- ☐ ..... Passports, Visas, Immunizations _________
- ☐ ..... Licenses, Permits __________________
- ☐ ..... Subway/Underground/Metro passes _____
- ☐ ..... Other transportation (cabs, trains) ______
- ☐ ..... Room __________________________
- ☐ ..... Food per day (estimated) _____________

  ____

- ☐ ..... Admission tickets (museums, parks, etc.) ___

  ____

- ☐ ..... Honeymoon Specials ________________
- ☐ ..... Special events ____________________

  ____

- ☐ ..... Restrictions (minimum stay) __________

  ____

Final Estimate

☐...... Destination ______________________________

☐...... From __________________ until ______________

☐...... Airfare per person ________________________

☐...... Car rental w/mileage charges ______________

☐...... Gasoline _________________________________

☐...... Airport shuttles ___________________________

☐...... Passports, Visas, Immunizations ___________

☐...... Licenses, Permits __________________________

☐...... Subway/Underground/Metro passes ______

☐...... Other transportation (cabs, trains) _________

☐...... Room ___________________________________

☐...... Food per day (estimated) __________________

____

☐...... Admission tickets (museums, parks, etc.) ____

____

☐...... Honeymoon Specials ______________________

☐...... Special events __________________________

____

☐...... Restrictions (minimum stay) ______________

____

First Estimate

- ☐ ..... Destination ______________________
- ☐ ..... From ______________ until ____________
- ☐ ..... Airfare per person ____________________
- ☐ ..... Car rental w/mileage charges ___________
- ☐ ..... Gasoline __________________________
- ☐ ..... Airport shuttles ______________________
- ☐ ..... Passports, Visas, Immunizations _________
- ☐ ..... Licenses, Permits _____________________
- ☐ ..... Subway/Underground/Metro passes ______
- ☐ ..... Other transportation (cabs, trains) ________
- ☐ ..... Room ____________________________
- ☐ ..... Food per day (estimated) ______________

____

- ☐ ..... Admission tickets (museums, parks, etc.) ___

____

- ☐ ..... Honeymoon Specials __________________
- ☐ ..... Special events ______________________

____

- ☐ ..... Restrictions (minimum stay) ____________

____

Second Estimate

☐...... Destination ______________________

☐...... From ______________ until ______________

☐...... Airfare per person ______________

☐...... Car rental w/mileage charges ______________

☐...... Gasoline ______________________

☐...... Airport shuttles ______________________

☐...... Passports, Visas, Immunizations ______________

☐...... Licenses, Permits ______________________

☐...... Subway/Underground/Metro passes ______

☐...... Other transportation (cabs, trains) ______________

☐...... Room ______________________

☐...... Food per day (estimated) ______________

____

☐...... Admission tickets (museums, parks, etc.) ____

____

☐...... Honeymoon Specials ______________

☐...... Special events ______________________

____

☐...... Restrictions (minimum stay) ______________

____

Third Estimate

☐ ..... Destination ______________________

☐ ..... From______________until____________

☐ ..... Airfare per person __________________

☐ ..... Car rental w/mileage charges __________

☐ ..... Gasoline__________________________

☐ ..... Airport shuttles ____________________

☐ ..... Passports, Visas, Immunizations_________

☐ ..... Licenses, Permits ___________________

☐ ..... Subway/Underground/Metro passes _____

☐ ..... Other transportation (cabs, trains) _______

☐ ..... Room ____________________________

☐ ..... Food per day (estimated) _____________

____

☐ ..... Admission tickets (museums, parks, etc.) ___

____

☐ ..... Honeymoon Specials________________

☐ ..... Special events _____________________

____

☐ ..... Restrictions (minimum stay) ___________

____

Fourth Estimate

- ☐...... Destination ____________________
- ☐...... From ____________ until ____________
- ☐...... Airfare per person ____________
- ☐...... Car rental w/mileage charges ____________
- ☐...... Gasoline ____________
- ☐...... Airport shuttles ____________
- ☐...... Passports, Visas, Immunizations ____________
- ☐...... Licenses, Permits ____________
- ☐...... Subway/Underground/Metro passes ____________
- ☐...... Other transportation (cabs, trains) ____________
- ☐...... Room ____________
- ☐...... Food per day (estimated) ____________

____

- ☐...... Admission tickets (museums, parks, etc.) ____

____

- ☐...... Honeymoon Specials ____________
- ☐...... Special events ____________

____

- ☐...... Restrictions (minimum stay) ____________

____

Getting Ready to Go

Home Security

☐☐. Have mail held starting________ending ____

(Start a few days early to make sure it works.)

☐☐. UPS (800-742-5877), FedEx (800-463-3339) asked to hold or forward packages (gifts) from _______to ________________________________

____

☐ ..... Put a hold on delivery services (e.g., water) _

from________________until ________________

☐☐. House watched by ________________

☐......Phone number ________________

☐☐. Pets watched by ________________

from________________until ________________

☐......Phone number ________________

☐☐. Children baby-sat by ________________

from________________until ________________

☐......Phone number ________________

☐☐. Timers set on lights in these rooms: ________

____

____

____

New timers have different settings for every day of the week or vary within 15 minutes of a set time to fool thieves. Confirm lights with timers aren't likely to fall over or be knocked (by pets) onto something flammable.

☐...... Valuables in safety deposit box at ____________

☐...... Fireplace flue closed (for warmth) ____________

☐...... Thermostat adjusted to save energy ________

☐...... Fix broken window or door locks ____________

☐...... Blinds adjusted. If you normally leave them all down, keep them all down; if you normally have them at all different heights, keep them at different heights so it looks normal - just make sure there's nothing valuable visible. Hide that Faberge Egg collection! ________________________________

____

____

____

____

____

____

____

____

International Travel

☐☐. Update passports two months before trip, by

______ on ________________________________

New passports cost more than renewals. You need two identical passport-size photos taken within the last six months, a birth certificate with a raised seal and a copy of your driver's license or other valid photo ID. It takes five or six weeks normally, but The National Passport Information Center can get you one in two weeks, for an extra fee. Large cities have passport centers with same-day service, for another fee. Some post offices accept applications.

☐...... Hers expires on ____________________

☐...... His expires on ____________________

☐☐. Get visas for both of you for (country and dates) ________________________________

____

____

☐☐. Get passport photos for passports, 2 each, and visas, 2 per person per visa.

☐...... Need total of_____photos of her _____

☐...... Need total of_____photos of him_____

☐ ..... Credit card companies notified of international travel so they don't think it's stolen and cut off your card. ____________________

☐...... Extra credit card in case of problems________

☐...... Buy $_______ in traveler's checks at ________

____

☐...... Buy travelers checks in foreign currency ____

AAA and some banks sell them to members.

☐...... Closest ATMs to hotel are located at ________

____

____

☐ ......Restrictions on usage (do you need a 4 digit pin for international use?) ___________

____

☐☐. Immunizations needed____________for_____

Most countries don't require them. ______________

____

☐...... Check health conditions with the Centers for Disease Control for more unusual spots. __________

____

☐...... Check the US State Department web site (travel.state.gov) or travel advisory line for potential hazards. ____________________________

____

____

Packing

Financial and related:

☐ ..... His cell phone charger____________________

☐ ..... Her cell phone charger ___________________

☐ ..... His laptop, tablet, Kindle and chargers _____

☐ ..... Her laptop, tablet, Kindle and chargers _____

☐☐. Cash and credit cards ____________________

☐ ..... List of credit card numbers and 800 numbers

____

☐ ..... Checking account number ________________

☐ ..... List of travelers check numbers ____________

☐ ..... Foreign currency ________________________

You can get it at a good rate from an ATM upon arrival.

☐ ..... Small calculator (for currency conversion) __

☐☐. His ____-___-___ and Her ____-___-___ SSN

☐ ..... His Driver's License state____ and #________

☐ ..... Her Driver's License state____ and #_______

____

Fun Stuff:

☐☐. Camera with new batteries, big memory card

☐...... Underwater camera (case)________________

☐...... Video recorder with extra tapes ____________

☐☐. Extra memory cards and batteries, chargers for still and video cameras ________________________

☐...... Massage oil. It's your honeymoon, and they aren't your sheets!____________________________

☐...... Lingerie! ____________________________

☐...... Lingerie! ____________________________

☐...... More Lingerie!__________________________

____

Medical:

☐...... Birth control___________________________

☐☐. Blood type: his____________her____________

☐...... He's allergic to__________________________

☐...... She's allergic to _________________________

☐...... Allergy medications _______________________

☐☐. Doctor's name and phone number__________

☐☐. Extra copies of prescriptions and medications

☐...... Motion sickness medication/wrist bands____

☐...... Advil/Tylenol ___________________________

☐☐. Sinutab/Sudafed__________________________

☐☐. Diarrhea/Constipation Medicine___________

____

Miscellaneous:

☐ ..... TSA approved lock and key for suitcase(s) __

☐ ..... Blank book for journal writing____________

☐ ..... Travel guides ____________________

☐ ..... Hotel phone number and address list_______

☐ ..... Address book ____________________

☐ ..... Postcard stamps __________________

☐ ..... List of people to buy gifts for ____________

☐ ..... Plastic bags for wet clothing/ toiletries______

☐☐. Swimsuits (for the beach or hotel)_________

☐☐. Travel pillows and gum _____________

____

____

____

Toiletries, etc.:

☐☐. Hair dryer, curling iron, rollers ___________

☐☐. Shampoo, conditioner _______________

☐☐. Hair gel, spray, etc. _________________

☐☐. Hair brush, comb ___________________

☐☐. Toothbrush, toothpaste ______________

☐☐. Shaving cream ______________________

☐☐. Razors ______________________

☐☐. Sunscreen (SPF______) ______________________

☐☐. Sunglasses ______________________

☐...... Make-up ______________________

☐...... Soap pouf or loufah ______________________

____

____

____

International travel:

☐...... Voltage converter ______________________

☐☐. Passport ______________________

☐☐. Visas ______________________

☐☐. International driver's license ______________________

☐☐. Immunization records ______________________

☐...... Foreign language dictionary ______________________

☐...... Insurance information ______________________

____

____

____

Paperwork

☐☐. Plane tickets ______________________________

☐☐. Passports _________________________________

☐☐. Copy 1st page of each passport (it makes replacing a lost passport much faster).

- ☐ ......One copy of each in luggage. ________
- ☐ ......One copy of each with someone at home. ______________________________

☐☐. Visas ______________________________________

____

☐☐. Copies of prescriptions ____________________

☐☐. Doctors phone numbers:

- ☐ ......His primary care physician__________
- ☐ ......Her primary care physician _________
- ☐ ......Gynecologist _____________________

☐☐. List of traveler's check numbers (take one along, leave one with _______________ at home) ____

____

- ☐ ......Both names on checks? ____________
- ☐ ......1st pad numbers____________to _____
- ....☐...Finished on_______ in __________
- ☐ ......2nd pad numbers____________to _____
- ....☐...Finished on_______ in __________

☐...... Credit card numbers and number to call if stolen:

☐ ......Card No.______________________________

Expiration________800-_______________________

☐ ......Card No.______________________________

Expiration________800-_______________________

☐ ......Card No.______________________________

Expiration________800-_______________________

☐ ......Card No.______________________________

Expiration________800-_______________________

☐ ......Card No.______________________________

Expiration________800-_______________________

☐ ......Card No.______________________________

Expiration________800-_______________________

☐...... Map printouts ___________________________

____

____

☐...... Directions / GPS_________________________

____

____

____

____

Phone Numbers & Addresses

☐ ..... Travel Agent ______________________

Phone number: ______________________

Address: ______________________

____

☐ ..... Car rental (for the ceremony) 800-__________

____

☐ ..... Car rental (for the honeymoon) 800-________

____

☐ ..... Hotel for night before wedding ____________

Phone number: ______________________

Address: ______________________

☐ ..... Honeymoon hotel #1: ____________________

Phone number: ______________________

Address: ______________________

☐ ..... Honeymoon hotel #2: ____________________

Phone number: ______________________

.... Address: ______________________

☐ ..... Shuttle **him** to airport ____________tel. _____

☐ ..... Shuttle **her** to airport ____________tel. ______

____

☐☐. Airline for wedding 800- ____________________

☐...... Shuttle **both** to airport ____________tel. _____

____

☐...... Airline for honeymoon 800- ________________

____

☐...... Baby-sitter ________________________________

____

☐...... Pet-sitter or kennel __________________________

____

☐...... Insurance companies ________________________

____

____

☐...... His parents___________________________________

____

☐...... Her parents ________________________________

____

☐...... Other_______________________________________

____

____

____

Final Confirmations

Two weeks before the honeymoon, by ____________ .

☐ ..... Car rental (for the ceremony) ______________

Rental agency and pick-up time: ___________

Confirmation number: ____________________

☐ ..... Car rental (for the honeymoon) ____________

Rental agency and pick-up time: ___________

Confirmation number: ____________________

☐ ..... Hotel for night before wedding ____________

Confirmation number: ____________________

Phone number: __________________________

Address: ________________________________

☐ ..... Honeymoon hotel #1: ____________________

Confirmation number: ____________________

Phone number: __________________________

Address: ________________________________

☐ ..... Honeymoon hotel #2: ____________________

Confirmation number: ____________________

Phone number: __________________________

Address: ________________________________

☐ ..... Shuttle **him** to fly to wedding picking up at (date, time & address) __________________________

Phone ______________ Confirmation # ____________

☐...... Shuttle **her** to fly to wedding picking up at (date, time & address) ________________________

Phone______________Confirmation #_____________

☐☐. Airplane reservations (wedding) __________

Departure city and time: ________________

Connecting city, arrival and departure time:

Destination arrival time: ________________

Airline and flight number(s): ____________

Confirmation number: __________________

☐...... Shuttle **both** to airport for honeymoon on ___

picking up at (time & address) _________________

Phone______________Confirmation #_____________

☐☐. Airplane reservations (honeymoon) ________

Departure airport and time: ______________

Connecting airport, arrival and departure time: ________________________________

Destination airport and arrival time:________

Airline and flight number(s): ____________

Confirmation number: __________________

☐...... Buy $_______ in traveler's checks at ________

☐...... Closest ATMs located at _______________

☐☐. Passports valid ________________________

☐☐. Visas valid, immunizations current_________

Wedding Night Hotel

- ☐ ..... Preferred locations ______________________

____

____

- ☐ ..... Amenities desired ______________________

____

____

- ☐ ..... Room size desired ______________________

____

- ☐ ..... First option ______________________
  - ☐ ...... Location ______________________
  - ☐ ...... Price ______________________
  - ☐ ...... Amenities ______________________
- ☐ ..... Second option ______________________
  - ☐ ...... Location ______________________
  - ☐ ...... Price ______________________
  - ☐ ...... Amenities ______________________
- ☐ ..... Third option ______________________
  - ☐ ...... Location ______________________
  - ☐ ...... Price ______________________
  - ☐ ...... Amenities ______________________

- [ ] ...... Fourth option ____________________
    - [ ] ......Location ____________________
    - [ ] ......Price ____________________
    - [ ] ......Amenities ____________________
- [ ] ...... Final choice: ____________________
    - [ ] ......Confirmation number ____________

Timelines

Every bridal magazine has them. Every wedding planner has them. This Organizer is no exception. I tried to be practical with what is included and how far in advance you should do it. Most wedding planners recommend that both moms start shopping for their dresses six months in advance. It can take quite a while to find the perfect Mother of the Bride / Groom dress, so starting to shop a full year in advance may make it less stressful for them. Plus, they have a better chance of finding a great dress on sale if they start a year in advance.

There are two pages for your actual wedding day, one for each of you. There are two reasons: (1) to make sure that you have enough time to do everything and (2) to remind you to do certain things, like eat breakfast. You might want to give it to your Honor Attendants.

There is also a page of what to do *after* your wedding. It's more than sending out thank-you notes. Among other things, you need to pick up your video, order photos (set aside several hours), and preserve/sell your gown. It's much less than you will do to plan your wedding, but you need to get it all done before you forget entirely.

The first things you must do are set a budget, decide on the formality of your wedding, and set a time frame for your wedding. Once you have a one (or two) month window, start looking at ceremony and reception sites. DO NOT DELAY LOOKING AT RECEPTION AND CEREMONY SITES. Reception sites are generally booked further in advance than ceremony sites and can generally only accommodate one wedding per day.

If you are marrying in a house of worship, meet with the officiant. They will tell you requirements and restrictions, as well as what they provide (dressing rooms, unity candleholder, Huppot).

After selecting a reception site, you should know your wedding date[4]. If you're getting married in a church or synagogue, call and confirm that you can use it the day and time you want.

The bride will probably want to start shopping for her gown too. You need to order her gown and bridesmaids' dresses AT LEAST six months in advance. If you take along ONE friend while you're shopping for your wedding dress and the bridesmaids' dresses, then you won't be overwhelmed by conflicting opinions.

Also, the bride should try on potential bridesmaids' dresses so you know how comfortable (or itchy) they are. If they are uncomfortable or look bad on you, then inflicting them on your bridesmaids is just not very nice.

---

[4] It seems somehow wrong that millions of wedding dates are decided by the availability of reception sites, but that's the way it is.

Exactly 1 Year Ahead

☐ ..... Mothers start shopping for their dresses.____

☐ ..... Visit a florist to see flowers (in-season = cheaper). ______________________________

____

☐ ..... Choose bridesmaids' dresses, especially if they are from a department store. _____________

6 Months to 1 Year Ahead

☐ ..... Buy this Wedding Organizer.____________

☐ ..... Announce your engagement in local papers. Many do not print them over 1 year ahead.________

____

☐ ..... Start exercising . Buy bridal magazines and carry them around. ______________________

☐ ..... Have your families meet. _______________

☐ ..... Discuss who will pay for what, and how much they can afford (see "Budget" sheets under "Basic Information") – giving you a Budget of $ ___

☐ ..... Determine wedding type and formality.

- ☐ ...... Formal, semi-formal, informal _______
- ☐ ...... Non-traditional types: themed (sports, western, historical), destination (guests travel to Scotland or Lake Tahoe for the wedding), ethnic, military.____________________

☐...... Choose a wedding consultant. ____________

☐...... Set a one-month time frame for your wedding. The final date may depend on reception site availability. ____________

☐...... Determine the ceremony location. ____________

____

☐...... Select a reception site. ____________

____

☐...... Set your wedding day. ____________

☐...... Select and meet with your officiants. ____________

- ☐ ......Reserve the ceremony site. ____________
- ☐ ......Check restrictions the site has (on secular music, birdseed, where to deliver flowers, hours). ____________

☐...... Choose your attendants. ____________

☐...... Draw up invitation lists:

- ☐ ......Yours____________# of guests ________
- ☐ ......Fiance's__________# of guests ________
- ☐ ......Her parents'_____# of guests ________
- ☐ ......His parents'_____# of guests ________

☐...... **Don't** register for gifts yet, despite what some books say. If you register too far ahead, items may be discontinued.

____

☐ ..... If you register early for engagement and shower gifts, register one place and update your registry after each party. Register more places later.

☐ ..... Select (good vendors book far in advance):

☐ ...... Bridal Gown!!! (at least 6 mos ahead)

____

☐ ...... Bustier, other undergarments ________

____

☐ ...... Headpiece and veil ________________

____

☐ ...... Bridal shoes _______________________

____

☐ ...... Color scheme ______________________

____

☐ ...... Bridesmaids' dresses (at least 6 months ahead) ___________________________

____

☐ ...... Photographer (candid / posed shots?)

____

☐ ...... Videographer ______________________

____

☐ ...... Florist ____________________________

____

____

- ☐ ......Baker ____________________
- ☐ ......Ceremony musician(s) ____________________
- ☐ ......Soloist ____________________
- ☐ ......Reception DJ/band ____________________

☐...... If you don't already, start exercising. ________

☐...... Develop a record-keeping system for invitations, gifts, thank-you notes, etc. ________

☐...... Determine what to have each mother help with, and what you don't want any "help" with. ___

4 to 6 Months Ahead

☐ ..... Begin attending counseling sessions with your officiant, if required.____________________

☐ ..... Check date bride will get her period the month of the wedding; if it's during the wedding or honeymoon, talk to ob/gyn about "rescheduling" it.

☐ ..... Order stationery. With mail order catalogs, you save on shipping and handling and may get other price breaks by ordering everything at once.

- ☐ ...... Invitations ____________________
  - ☐ ... Lined inner envelopes ________
- ☐ ... Outer envelopes w/return address ____
  - ☐ ... Response cards _____________
  - ☐ ... Reception cards _____________
  - ☐ ... Stickers to seal them (worth it) __
- ☐ ...... Personal stationery and notepaper ___
- ☐ ...... Thank you notes ________________
- ☐ ...... Cocktail napkins, matchbooks ______
- ☐ ...... Thank you scrolls, cake boxes ______

☐ ..... Buy ___Forever stamps for thank you notes, responses ______________________________

☐ ..... Buy _______stamps at ____ ¢ for invites_____

☐ ..... Check state marriage license requirements __

☐ ..... Plan your honeymoon__________________

☐...... Shop for going-away outfit[5]. ______________

☐...... Have a complete physical, set blood test date, and immunizations for your honeymoon. _________

☐ ......Have your fiancé do the same. ________

☐☐. Get passports, visas ______________________

☐...... Check with the bridal shop to verify when bridal gown and bridesmaids' dresses will arrive. __

☐...... Select a hotel for out-of-town guests and reserve a block of rooms at a reduced rate _________

☐...... Buy ring bearer pillow, guest book, etc. _____

☐...... Select wedding rings, request engraving:

☐ ......His: size_______, engraved __________

☐ ......Hers: size______, engraved __________

☐...... Enroll with bridal registries; update existing registries. Include one national registry __________

☐...... Update registr(ies) after each shower _______

☐...... Reserve rehearsal dinner site ______________

☐...... Reserve groom's tuxedo (it's often free) _____

☐...... Select attendants' gifts (his)________________

☐...... Select attendants' gifts (hers) ______________
____

[5] You won't ever wear your wedding gown out to a regular dinner, but you can wear your going-away outfit out and about.

2 to 4 Months Ahead

☐ ..... (e)Mail Wedding Party Information Packets _

☐ ..... Address wedding invitations. Have a party with your attendants so they can help.____________

☐ ..... Set a date with your fiancé to get your marriage license. If you are in another state, ask the County Clerk if a waiver is available to get it closer to the wedding.________________________________

☐ ..... Confirm you meet all religious requirements.

☐ ..... Alter / dry clean bridal gown. ____________

☐ ..... Decide if you or your guests need baby-sitting services and arrange for them.____________

☐ ..... Arrange for wedding day limousine. _______

☐ ..... Decide on favors. ______________________

☐ ..... Buy a wedding gift for your fiancé.________

☐ ..... Send GPS-able addresses for:

- ☐ ...... Hotel for out of town guests_________
- ☐ ...... Rehearsal location _______________
- ☐ ...... Rehearsal dinner location __________
- ☐ ...... Ceremony location________________
- ☐ ...... Reception location ________________

☐ ..... Mail international invitations______________

☐ ..... Decide when/if to have a bridesmaids' party, then plan it ________________________________

☐...... Shop for trousseau ______________________

☐...... Ask more friends to assist in your wedding:

- ☐ ......Guest book attendant ______________
- ☐ ......Acolyte(s) ______________________
- ☐ ......Reader(s) ______________________
- ☐ ......Bulletin/birdseed distributors _______
- ☐ ......Huppot pole holders ______________
- ☐ ......Set up/check the reception site ______

☐...... Select ceremony music (see page under Ceremony / Reception tab for all music) __________

☐...... Select reception music ________________

☐...... Hairstylist appointments:

- ☐ ......Pre-wedding ______________________
- ☐ ......Wedding Day _____________________

☐...... Make-up appointments, stylist and colors you like. Use the same ones your wedding day.

- ☐ ......Pre-wedding appointment __________
- ☐ ......Wedding day appointment __________
- ☐ ......Stylist ___________________________
- ☐ ......Foundation, blush __________________
- ☐ ......Eyeshadow(s) _____________________
- ☐ ......Lipstick/gloss/liner ________________
- ☐ ......Mascara/eyeliner __________________

1 to 2 Months Ahead

☐ ..... GET PASSPORTS AND VISAS ____________

☐ ..... Get your marriage license ____________

☐ ..... Final dress fitting on ____________

☐ ..... Plan how to handle traffic, parking ____________

☐ ..... Mail invitations ____________

☐ ..... Make sure attendants ordered their clothing or reserved rental clothing ____________

☐ ..... Have a formal wedding portrait done ______

☐ ..... Pick up wedding rings ____________

☐ ..... Shop for your trousseau ____________

☐ ..... Write your wedding program/bulletin ______

☐ ..... Write your vows, if you are doing so ______

☐ ..... Select readings for the ceremony:

____

____

☐ ..... Take dance classes ____________

☐ ..... Make a list of must-have and would-like photos ____________

____

☐ ..... Make a list of must-have and would-like video moments ____________

☐...... Finish assembling favors. (Do you really want to do this the night before your wedding?) Ask attendants to help. ______________________

☐...... Get the necessary name-change documents, if needed. ______________________________

☐...... Finish assembling/decorating birdseed or bubbles, or empty a bag of birdseed into a pretty basket and have guests take a handful to throw.____

☐...... Reserve wedding night hotel room for **late arrival** (after 6 pm). _________________________

☐...... Make honeymoon reservations for:

- ☐ ......Airline_________________________
- ☐ ......Airport shuttle from reception _______
- ☐ ......Airport shuttle to/from hotel/resort__
- ☐ ......Hotel/resort______________________
- ☐ ......Special events (shows, tours, etc.) ____
- ☐ ......Rental car _______________________

☐...... Wedding gift purchased for your fiancé_____

☐...... Attendants' gifts are purchased - his________

☐...... Attendants' gifts are purchased - hers_______

☐...... Have a pre-nuptial agreement written ______

☐...... Look at the ceremony site dressing room – does it have an iron/ironing board, mirrors? ______

____

2 Weeks Ahead

☐ ..... GET YOUR MARRIAGE LICENSE________

☐ ..... Pay all your regular bills________________

☐ ..... Send wedding announcements to the local papers____

☐ ..... Finalize seating arrangements, write placecards ________________________________

☐ ..... Final bridal gown fitting________________

☐ ..... Proofread your bulletins/programs ________

____

☐ ..... Copy your bulletins/programs ___________

____

☐ ..... Gather together anything you'll need for your honeymoon that's packed away -- voltage converter, swimsuits/coats and other off-season clothing -- and put it in your suitcase(s). _________

____

☐ ..... Wrap your attendants' thank you gifts______

☐ ..... Keep writing thank you notes ____________

☐ ..... Have mail held while you're away _________

☐ ..... Give copies of reception program to DJ/Master of Ceremonies and Reception Host/Hostess ______________________________

Final Meetings - 2 Weeks Ahead

☐...... Officiant ______________________________

☐...... Baker – give them the cake topper __________

☐...... Caterer ________________________________

☐...... Reception site __________________________

____

☐...... Rehearsal dinner site ____________________

☐...... Videographer – tell them any special requests ______________________________________

☐...... Photographer – tell them any special requests

____

☐...... Hairdresser ____________________________

☐...... Make-up artist __________________________

☐...... Your fiancé – nothing wedding related! **Especially** if you don't think you have the time.____

____

☐...... Florist _________________________________

☐...... Wedding coordinator ______________________

☐☐. Attendants (his and hers) _________________

☐...... Your children - not wedding related! _______

____

2 Weeks Ahead - Final Confirmations

☐ ..... Car rental (for the ceremony) ______________

☐ ..... Car rental (for the honeymoon) ____________

☐ ..... Wedding hotel for bridal party ____________

☐ ......Number of rooms reserved__________

☐ ..... Cancel extra rooms held by credit card on___

____

☐ ..... Wedding night hotel confirmed for **late arrival** (after 6 pm)___________________________

____

☐ ..... Honeymoon hotel(s) ______________________

____

☐☐. Airplane reservations (wedding)___________

____

☐☐. Airplane reservations (honeymoon) ________

____

☐ ..... Guest count in by ________________________

☐☐. Haircut and styled _______________________

☐ ..... Make-up appointment_____________________

☐ ..... Gown still fits (with shoes & undergarments)

____

☐...... Manicure appointment ____________________

☐...... Pedicure appointment ____________________

☐...... Ceremony site reserved for rehearsal _______

____

☐...... Rehearsal dinner site reserved _____________

____

☐...... Baker has cake topper and is delivering cake

at____:_____to _____________________________

☐☐. Ring sizes: his____________hers___________

☐☐. Rings fit and engraving is correct___________

☐☐. Have mail held ___________________________

☐☐. House watched ___________________________

☐☐. Pets watched _____________________________

☐☐. Children baby-sat _________________________

☐☐. Timers set on your home(s)_______________

____

☐...... Pre-nuptial agreement finished ____________

____

☐...... Confirm parking arrangements with the ceremony and reception sites.________________

____

1 Week Ahead

☐ ..... **GET YOUR MARRIAGE LICENSE.** ________

☐ ..... Prepare announcements for mailing, then give them to someone to mail the day after the wedding. ________

☐ ..... IF YOU'RE GETTING A COLD, take Echinacea, Zinc Lozenges, Airborne™ – whatever helps you. ________

☐ ..... Finalize seating plan. ________

☐ ..... Have final consultations (via phone?) with:

- ☐ ...... Caterer ________
- ☐ ...... Florist ________
- ☐☐ . Photographer, videographer ________
- ☐ ...... Officiant ________

☐ ..... Start packing for your honeymoon ________

☐ ..... Give a bridesmaids' party ________

☐ ..... Confirm rental tux style and arrival date and time. ________

☐ ..... Confirm rehearsal plans with:

- ☐ ...... Officiant ________
- ☐ ...... Attendants ________
- ☐ ...... Family members ________

☐ ..... Confirm hairdresser appointment(s) ________

☐ ..... Confirm make-up artist appointment(s) ____

- ☐...... Give caterer final guest count on ____________
- ☐...... Confirm travel arrangements:
  - ☐ ......To the wedding ______________________
  - ☐ ......Your honeymoon ____________________
- ☐...... **Stop** writing thank you notes until after your wedding; use any free time to relax _________________
- ☐...... Get a last-minute hair trim __________________
- ☐...... Assemble everything to:
  - ☐ ......Take to the rehearsal _________________
  - ☐ ......Take to the ceremony site ____________
  - ☐ ......Take to the reception site (favors, etc.)
  - ☐ ......Give attendants ______________________
  - ☐ ......Keep in bridal emergency bag ________
- ☐...... Gather your wedding clothing:
  - ☐ ......Bustier/bra, underwear _______________
  - ☐ ......Garters, stockings/nylons ____________
  - ☐ ......Shoes ____________________________
  - ☐ ......Make-up __________________________
  - ☐ ......Necklace, bracelet, earrings___________
  - ☐ ......Headpiece, veil _____________________
- ☐...... Buy a good, easy-to-read book or non-bridal magazine to read when you can't sleep (or wake up at dawn) the night before your wedding. ___________

1 Day Ahead

☐ ..... CONFIRM THAT YOU HAVE YOUR MARRIAGE LICENSE ____________________

____

☐ ..... Get a manicure ____________________

____

☐ ..... Get a pedicure____________________

____

☐ ..... Gather non-bridal wedding day clothing:

- ☐ ......Button-down shirt to wear to hair and make-up appointments so your hair and make-up don't get mussed. ____________
- ☐ ......Headpiece/veil to take to hairdresser appointment.____________________
- ☐ ......Going away outfit - including shoes, socks, undergarments and jewelry.__________

____

____

____

____

____

____

☐...... Finish packing for your honeymoon. ________

☐...... Attend rehearsal dinner. ________

☐...... Draft anyone who comes near you to help with whatever you need. ________

☐...... Socialize. ________

☐...... Take a good, easy-to-read book or non-bridal magazine to bed for when you're wide awake at 3 am, 4 am,.... (It's better than counting sheep -- and you can re-read it when you're less distracted.) ________

Your Wedding Day!!! (Bride)

(Fill in approximate times in advance.)

: .... Get up ______________________________

: .... Eat breakfast __________________________

: .... Finish last-minute honeymoon packing_____

: .... Shower, shave, etc.______________________

: .... Have your hair done ____________________

: .... Have your make-up done_________________

: .... Eat__________________________________

: .... Honor attendant arrives _________________

: .... Bridesmaids arrive_____________________

: .... Go to the bathroom while it's still easy _____

(Put on your bustier 15-20 minutes before your gown so you can "settle" into it a bit before dressing.)

: .... Dress________________________________

: .... Limo takes you to ceremony site __________

: .... Photos start ___________________________

: .... Ceremony starts ________________________

: .... Photos resume _________________________

: .... Reception starts ________________________

: .... Reception ends _________________________

: .... Depart for your honeymoon ______________

: .... Post-reception party with out of town guests

: ... Flight departs ______________________

Your Wedding Day!!! (Groom)

(Fill in the approximate times in advance.)

: ... Get up ______________________

: ... Eat breakfast ______________________

: ... Finish last-minute honeymoon packing _____

: ... Shower, shave, etc. ______________________

: ... Pack toiletries ______________________

: ... Get dressed ______________________

: ... Best Man arrives ______________________

: ... Pick up rental car (if necessary) ____________

: ... Eat ______________________

: ... Put on tux ______________________

: ... Groomsmen arrive ______________________

: ... Go to ceremony site ______________________

: .... Go to the bathroom while you have time ____

: ... Photos start ______________________

: ... Ceremony starts ______________________

: ... Photos resume ______________________

: ... Reception starts ______________________

: ... Reception ends ______________________

: ... Depart for your honeymoon ______________

: ... Post-reception party with out of town guests

: .... Flight departs ______________________________

Within 1-2 Months AFTER

☐ ..... Photographer: see page under "Vendors". ___

☐ ..... Select newspaper announcement photos. ___

____

☐ ..... Submit newspaper announcements. ________

☐ ..... Order ____copies of your certified marriage certificate from the County Clerk (for banks, social security, etc. to change your name). ____________

☐ ..... Open your gifts!!! We invited friends who lived nearby for a mini-party. It was a nice chance to socialize, and they recorded who gave us what so we could focus on opening. We also ate the top layer of our cake. _____________________

☐ ..... Update registries to reflect gifts you've received. You'll get a few more wedding gifts and family can buy holiday/birthday gifts from your registry. ______________________________

☐ ..... Wedding gown:

- ☐ ......Pick up from cleaners ___________
- ☐ ......Have it preserved_______________
- ☐ ......Take to consignment store ________
- ☐ ......Hang in parents' closet for 20 years __

☐ ..... Buy extra photo albums. _______________

☐ ..... Wedding and honeymoon photos put in albums.______________________________

☐...... **Thank you notes** sent within <u>three months</u> of return from honeymoon. For gifts of money, describing what you're buying makes writing notes easier.

☐ ......Attendants (for being in the wedding, gifts, and anything specific they helped with)

☐☐ .Immediate family ________________

☐☐ .Extended family ________________

☐☐ .Bride and groom's friends __________

☐☐ .Parents' friends ________________

☐☐ .Coworkers, neighbors of bride and groom

☐☐ .Coworkers, neighbors of parents _____

☐...... Videographer:

..........☐ ......Pick up final copy of video on _______

..........☐ ......Master tape kept until _____________

..........☐ ......Cost to buy master tape ___________

☐...... Wedding announcement in newspapers:

..........☐☐ .His/her hometown________________

..........☐☐ .Current local paper_______________

____

____

____

Name Change

☐ ..... Social Security ______________________

☐ ..... Car registration ______________________

☐ ..... Driver's license ______________________

☐ ..... Car title(s) ______________________

☐ ..... Passport ______________________

☐ ..... Voter registration ______________________

☐ ..... Bank(s) - checking, savings, loans - add spouse?:

☐☐ ______________________

☐☐ ______________________

☐☐ ______________________

☐ ..... Student, other loans ______________________

☐ ..... Credit cards:

☐ ______________________

☐ ______________________

☐ ______________________

☐☐. IRA, 401K, other investments ______________________

☐ ..... Update lease or mortgage ______________________

☐ ..... Will ______________________

☐☐. College/university(s) alumni association ___

☐ ..... Employer ______________________

- ☐ ......Employee records ____________________
- ☐ ......Letterhead paper ____________________
- ☐ ......Business cards ____________________
- ☐ ......Email address ____________________
- ☐ ......Phone directory listing ____________________

☐ ...... Insurance company(s):

- ☐ ____________________
- ☐ ____________________

☐ ...... Beneficiaries ____________________

____

____

☐ ...... Safety deposit box ____________________

☐ ...... Post office ____________________

☐ ...... Primary care physician ____________________

☐ ...... OB/Gyn ____________________

☐ ...... Eye doctor ____________________

☐ ...... Dentist ____________________

☐ ...... Other doctor ____________________

☐☐ . Magazines, newspaper ____________________

☐ ...... Club(s): ____________________

____

Vendors

For your wedding, you will need to select quite a few vendors. These include the photographer, florist, videographer, reception site (see "Ceremony & Reception" section), musicians, baker, and more.

Make certain you tell vendors what matters most to you (preferably in writing) before the wedding and reiterate it on your wedding day, if necessary. In all the rushing around, sometimes even professionals forget. I absolutely insisted that photos and video be taken of our flower girls in my parent's yard. They were beautiful and meant a lot more to the family than a picture anywhere else could have.

You may choose to preserve the bridal bouquet from your wedding. Do-it-yourself methods include pressing, hanging/drying, and making potpourri. It is also possible to send your bouquet to a professional preservationist. They advertise in major bridal magazines. If you are interested in this, get brochures from each company. They have different methods for drying your flowers and then putting them in wall hangings, shadow boxes or acrylic boxes to set on a table. It's not cheap, but it's for the rest of your life and you probably spent a lot of time and money on your bridal bouquet for one day. Of course, if you don't think you'll want to display it, save your money.

If you have a Sunday wedding, verify that each vendor will work and deliver on Sunday.

Hints and Tips

- You will probably have more of your family gathered together than you have had in a long time. Don't be afraid to ask the photographer to take a few family portraits. We had pictures of each of our parents with their parents and siblings, and a second one with the siblings spouses. My cousins want copies. Just remember, unless you really stress that they are important and tell family members to seek out the photographer, they may be forgotten in the rush of events. The photographer knows who you are, but she doesn't know Aunt Gertrude.

- Remember, **these people work for you**; they are here for your convenience, not the other way around. Don't let a photographer drag you outside during dinner because "the lighting is perfect" if dinner is important to you. But don't let the caterer guilt you into finishing dinner and missing the "perfect lighting" if photos are critical to you.

- Have someone bring drinks to the bridal party during any photo shoots and make sure the caterer sends waiters out with drinks and appetizers. You probably won't even have time to stop at a water fountain. Seriously.

- When you order your wedding album, remember that all of your professional photos don't have to go in an album from the photographer. Archival quality albums cost and weigh less than professional albums and still preserve your photos. You can put some in a professional album and order more loose to put in a less expensive album.

- Professional photos are usually copyright protected, so it is illegal to make extra copies of them yourself. You will need to pay the photographer unless you have their express permission to make copies or you have bought the original files.
- Check the vendors your parents used if you're getting married in the same area. If a photography studio is still in business after 30 or 40 years, they're probably good. You'll still need to ask lots of questions, and you may not like the studio, but it's pretty cool if you do!

Notes

Invitations and Other Stationery

- ☐ ..... Store or catalog ____________________
  - ☐ ...... Address ____________________
  - ☐ ...... Website ____________________
  - ☐ ...... Phone number ____________________
  - ☐ ...... Order confirmation number ____________________
  - ☐ ...... Delivery date ____________________

____

____

- ☐ ..... Invitations and enclosures:
  - ☐ ...... Style ordered ____________________
  - ☐ ...... Inner envelopes ____________________
  - ☐ ...... Lining color ____________________
  - ☐ ...... Outer envelopes ____________________
  - ☐ ...... Printed flaps (worth it) ____________________
  - ☐ ...... Invitation ____________________
  - ☐ ...... RSVP with envelope ____________________
  - ☐ ...... Send RSVP to ____________________
  - ☐ ...... Envelope seals (also worth it) ____________________
  - ☐ ...... Directions to wedding ____________________

____

____

- [ ] ......Directions to reception ______________

____

____

- [ ] ......Hotel information ______________

____

- [ ] ...... Informal notes ______________
- [ ] ...... Announcements ______________
- [ ] ...... Thank you notes (shower) ______________

____

- [ ] ...... Thank you notes (wedding) ______________

____

- [ ] ...... Personal stationery ______________
- [ ] ...... Placecards ______________
- [ ] ...... Thank you scrolls ______________
- [ ] ...... Bookmarks ______________
- [ ] ...... Napkins ______________
- [ ] ...... Matchbooks ______________
- [ ] ...... Other ______________

____

____

Florist

☐ ..... Colors (to avoid clashing): attendants ______

ceremony__________and reception sites __________

☐ ..... Florist name ______________________________

☐ ..... Address __________________________________

☐ ..... Phone number ____________________________

☐ ..... Time and location of delivery ____________

☐☐. Bridal and toss bouquets__________________

☐ ..... Preservation of bridal bouquet ____________

☐ ..... Maid of Honor ____________________________

☐ ..... Bridesmaids ______________________________

☐ ..... Jr. Bridesmaids ___________________________

☐ ..... Flower girls _______________________________

☐ ..... Wreaths, sprays, etc. for hair ______________

☐ ..... Groom ___________________________________

☐ ..... Best Man _________________________________

☐ ..... Groomsmen________________________________

☐ ..... Jr. Groomsmen ____________________________

☐ ..... Ushers ___________________________________

☐ ..... Ring bearer ______________________________

☐ ..... Guest book attendant ______________________

☐☐. Mothers (gown colors________) ____________

☐☐. Fathers ____________________

☐☐☐☐..Grandmothers ____________________

☐☐☐☐..Grandfathers ____________________

☐☐. Godparents ____________________

☐☐. Special family members____________________

☐...... Organist/musician ____________________

☐...... Other (officiant doesn't get one)____________

☐...... Reception decorations ____________________

☐...... Altar (take them to the reception or leave them at the church?) or Huppot flowers____________

☐☐. Pew markers ____________________

☐...... Candelabras____________________

☐...... Aisle runner (florists often provide them) ___

☐...... Kneeler ____________________

☐...... Potted flowers ____________________

☐...... Table centerpieces and garlands:

- ☐ ......Bridal table____________________
- ☐ ......Parent's table ____________________
- ☐ ......Guest tables ____________________

☐...... Cake top (baker gets these) ____________

☐☐. Guest book stand, cake table______________

Florist Estimates

Estimate #1

☐ ..... Company name ______________________

☐ ..... Address ____________________________

☐ ..... Phone number (_____)_________________

☐ ..... Website ____________________________

☐ ..... Bridal bouquet / toss bouquet ___________

☐ ..... Bridesmaids' flowers __________________

☐ ..... Boutonnieres _________________________

☐ ..... Altar flowers _________________________

☐ ..... Table centerpieces ____________________

☐ ..... Misc. flower _________________________

☐ ..... Delivery and set-up ___________________

Estimate #2

☐ ..... Company name ______________________

☐ ..... Address ____________________________

☐ ..... Phone number (_____)_________________

☐ ..... Website ____________________________

☐ ..... Bridal bouquet / toss bouquet ___________

☐ ..... Bridesmaids' flowers __________________

☐ ..... Boutonnieres _________________________

☐...... Altar flowers ______________________________

☐...... Table centerpieces___________________________

☐...... Misc. flower _______________________________

☐...... Delivery and set-up _______________________

Estimate #3

☐...... Company name___________________________

☐...... Address _________________________________

☐...... Phone number (_____) ____________________

☐...... Website___________________________________

☐...... Bridal bouquet / toss bouquet _____________

☐...... Bridesmaids' flowers ______________________

☐...... Boutonnieres _____________________________

☐...... Altar flowers ______________________________

☐...... Table centerpieces___________________________

☐...... Misc. flower _______________________________

☐...... Delivery and set-up _______________________

____

____

____

____

____

Photographer

- ☐ ..... Photographer's name on contract __________
- ☐ ..... Studio name ____________________________
- ☐ ..... Phone number __________________________
- ☐ ..... Engagement/announcement photo on______
- ☐ ..... Wedding day arrival/departure time_______
- ☐ ..... Where will they arrive____________________
- ☐ ..... Proofs ready on _________________________
- ☐ ..... Original files kept until ___________________
- ☐ ..... Can you buy original files later? ___________
- ☐ ..... Can you get black and white photos too? ___
- ☐ ..... Order deadline________for delivery on _____
- ☐ ..... Select photos for:
  - ☐☐ . Newspaper announcements_________
    - ☐ ..Color ______________________
    - ☐ ..Black and white ________________
  - ☐☐☐☐ ..Parents _____________________
  - ☐☐☐☐ ..Grandparents ________________
  - ☐☐ . Other gifts _________________________
  - ☐ ...... Your photo album __________________
  - ☐☐ . 5x7 and 8x10 photos for home and office .

☐...... Select photo album and mats ______________

☐...... Personalization for album cover____________

☐...... Prices:

- ☐ ......Proofs (can you buy print proofs if they don't use them?)____________________$
- ☐ ......4 x 5____________________$
- ☐ ......5 x 7____________________$
- ☐ ......8 x 10____________________$
- ☐ ......11 x 14____________________$
- ☐ ......16 x 20____________________$
- ☐ ......Wallets ____________________$
- ☐ ......Price breaks for large purchases______

____

☐...... Total amount for package _________________

☐...... Amount of package cost applied toward album. ____

☐...... Delivery date __________________________

Archival quality albums do not damage photos, even after many years. Albums with plastic sleeves (like archival albums) also use less space. We needed albums for table camera pictures, honeymoon photos, and professional photos we ordered loose. All the professional photos do not have to be in one album.

Photographer Estimates

Estimate #1

☐ ..... Company name ______________________

☐ ..... Photographer's name__________________

The person who will photograph your wedding. Look at samples of their work and put their name in the contract.

☐ ..... Address ____________________________

☐ ..... Phone number (_____)_________________

☐ ..... Website ____________________________

☐ ..... Basic cost is $__________ for ____(#) cameras and a photographer with/without an assistant. ____

for _____hours,_____photos; extra hours cost $ ____

☐ ..... Basic package includes _____(#) photos_____

☐ ..... Proofs available ____weeks after wedding __

____

Estimate #2

☐ ..... Company name ______________________

☐ ..... Photographer's name__________________

The person who will photograph your wedding. Look at samples of their work and put their name in the contract.

☐ ..... Address ____________________________

☐...... Phone number (_____) ____________________

☐...... Website ________________________________

☐...... Basic cost is $__________ for ____(#) cameras and a photographer with/without an assistant. ____

for _____hours,_____photos; extra hours cost $_____

☐...... Basic package includes _____(#) photos _____

☐...... Proofs available ____weeks after wedding___

____

Estimate #3

☐...... Company name ___________________________

☐...... Photographer's name ______________________

The person who will photograph <u>your wedding</u>. Look at samples of <u>their work</u> and put <u>their name</u> in the contract.

☐...... Address ________________________________

☐...... Phone number (_____) ____________________

☐...... Website ________________________________

☐...... Basic cost is $__________ for ____(#) cameras and a photographer with/without an assistant. ____

for _____hours,_____photos; extra hours cost $_____

☐...... Basic package includes _____(#) photos _____

☐...... Proofs available ____weeks after wedding___

Special Photo Requests

Ours included: my nieces in "their" flower gardens at my parents' house, a "trick" shot of Mom and me in her wedding gown (which I wore), and the cake baker and Mom (childhood friends) with the cake.

Photographers have a standard list of shots they take, but you should give them a list of anything special. Make sure they know if there are any you ABSOLUTELY WANT taken. They work for you.

☐ ..... First dance – if you take lessons, tell them. Also tell them if it's choreographed so they know when fancy moves like dips occur in the song. _____

____

☐☐. Father with his parents, siblings ___________

____

☐☐. Mother with her parents, siblings __________

____

☐☐. Multi-generational shots (great-grandma, grandmother, mother, you, sister-in-law, nieces) ___

____

____

☐ ..... Outdoor location(s) ____________________

____

☐...... Group shots of kids ______________________

____

☐...... Special ceremony participants ______________

____

☐...... Special moments (reading by a family member, song by a friend, other personalized moments) ______________________________________

____

____

____

____

____

____

____

____

____

____

____

____

____

Videographer

Estimate #1

☐ ..... Company Name ______________________

☐ ..... Videographer's name ________________

The person who would actually tape your wedding. You should see samples of their work and include their name in your contract.

☐ ..... Address ____________________________

☐ ..... Phone number (_____)_________________

☐ ..... Website ____________________________

☐ ..... Basic cost is $__________ for ____(#) cameras and a videographer with/without an assistant for __________hours, extra hours cost $ ____________

☐ ..... Basic package includes ___(#) copies of video

☐ ..... Cost for additional copies ________________

☐ ..... Master tape is/is not included ____________

☐ ..... Finished video available ____weeks after wedding_______________________________________

☐ ..... Types of videos available ________________

☐ ..... Special effects available_________________

____

☐ ..... Standard shots included _________________

____

Estimate #2

☐...... Company Name ______________________

☐...... Videographer name __________________

The person who would actually tape your wedding. You should see samples of their work and include their name in your contract.

☐...... Address ____________________________

☐...... Phone number (_____) ________________

☐...... Website_____________________________

☐...... Basic cost is $__________ for ____(#) cameras and a videographer with/without an assistant for __________hours, extra hours cost $ ____________

☐...... Basic package includes ___(#) copies of video

☐...... Cost for additional copies _______________

☐...... Master tape is/is not included ____________

☐...... Finished video available ____weeks after wedding_____________________________________

☐...... Types of videos available _______________

☐...... Special effects available _________________

____

☐...... Standard shots included _______________

____

____

Special Video Requests

☐ ..... Special moments (reading by a family member, song by a friend, other personalized moments)____________________________

____

____

____

☐ ..... First dance – if you take lessons, tell them. Also tell them if it's choreographed; they should know when fancy moves like dips occur in the song.

____

☐ ..... Video messages. The more you request, the greater the likelihood they won't get them all, and the less footage you'll get of other moments.

- ☐☐ . Parents ____________________
- ☐☐☐☐ .. Grandparents _______________
- ☐☐☐☐ .. Siblings ____________________
- ☐☐ . Your children _________________
- ☐☐ . His aunts and uncles ______________
- ☐☐ . Her aunts and uncles ______________
- ☐☐ . Favorite cousins _______________
- ☐ ...... Bridal party __________________
- ☐☐ . College friends ________________

☐☐ .Other friends ____________________

____

☐...... "Pan" guests during pre-ceremony music ___

____

☐...... Footage of musicians performing__________

____

Your Marriage

Your wedding day is the first day of your married life. It's your first day as a wife or a husband. It's the biggest party in your honor that you will probably ever have.

Your wedding is not like of the rest of your life.

From the moment you say "yes" through your wedding day, everyone will focus on you. If you're the bride, they will ask about your dress and all the arrangements and admire your engagement ring. If you're the groom, they will be amazed that you're really involved in planning your wedding and will ask about her engagement ring. People will listen to you obsess over every detail down to napkin rings and the virtues of engraved versus unengraved cake knives.

This will not continue past the wedding. It can be quite a shock to go from having everyone ask you about all your plans and being the center of attention to being just another married person. This is when your marriage starts. This is necessarily not happy change for many people, even though they're thrilled to be married to the love of their life. It can be a huge change to go from being the center of attention and busily planning The Big Day, to being a regular person busy with normal household chores, or having an empty vacuum of time to fill.

If you (both of you) spend some time thinking about the things you want *after* the wedding and honeymoon are over even *before* the wedding, then you can start working toward those things as you finish your thank you notes, name changing, and other post-wedding obligations.

Think about what you spend your time on right now. How much of it is the wedding? What will you do with that large chunk of time after the wedding? Going to movies? Shopping? Watching TV reruns? Planning your future? Watching TV reruns *while* planning your future?

This section does not include all of the things you and your fiancé should talk about related to your future hopes and dreams. It won't help you make sure you have enough money to retire early or take great trips. It will, ideally, get you two to talk about your hopes and dreams for your new family. After this, hopefully you will both have the same expectations for how much you should be saving for retirement versus spending on great trips, among other things.

No one can wave a magic wand and cause you to get along with your new mother-in-law (or your own mother), but maybe discussing these things will ease a few of the potential problems. More importantly, they will help ensure that you and your new spouse are on the same page planning your lives together.

Medical History

☐ ..... Blood type: His____________ Her __________

☐ ..... His food allergies ________________________

____

☐ ..... His medicine allergies ____________________

____

☐ ..... His other allergies _______________________

____

☐ ..... His chronic medical problems _____________

____

____

____

☐ ..... His hospitalizations / surgeries___________

____

____

☐ ..... His childhood illnesses ___________________

____

____

☐ ..... His family history of medical problems _____

____

____

____

☐ ......Cancer ______________________________

____

☐ ......Heart conditions ______________________________

____

☐ ......Stroke ______________________________

____

☐ ......Mental health ______________________________

____

☐ ......Other ______________________________

☐ ...... His primary care physician ______________________________

☐ ......Telephone ______________________________

☐ ...... His dentist ______________________________

☐ ......Telephone ______________________________

☐ ...... His eye doctor ______________________________

☐ ......Telephone ______________________________

☐ ...... His other doctor ______________________________

☐ ......Telephone ______________________________

____

☐ ...... Her food allergies ______________________________

____

☐ ..... Her medicine allergies ____________________

____

☐ ..... Her other allergies ______________________

____

☐ ..... Her chronic medical problems ____________

____

____

☐ ..... Her hospitalizations / surgeries __________

____

☐ ..... His major illnesses ______________________

____

☐ ..... Her major illnesses ______________________

____

☐ ..... Her childhood illnesses ___________________

____

☐ ..... Her family history of medical problems _____

☐ ...... Cancer ___________________________

____

☐ ...... Heart conditions ____________________

____

☐ ......Stroke ______________________________

____

☐ ......Mental health________________________

____

☐ ......Other________________________________

____

☐...... Her ob/gyn history ____________________

____

☐...... Her ob/gyn ___________________________

☐ ......Telephone_____________________________

☐...... Her primary care physician______________

☐ ......Telephone_____________________________

☐...... Her dentist ____________________________

☐ ......Telephone_____________________________

☐...... Her eye doctor__________________________

☐ ......Telephone_____________________________

☐...... Her other doctor ________________________

☐ ......Telephone_____________________________

____

____

Fitness / Diet

☐ ..... Her food allergies ____________________

____

☐ ..... His food allergies ____________________

____

☐ ..... Foods she LOVES ____________________

____

☐ ..... Foods he LOVES ____________________

____

☐ ..... Foods she WILL NOT eat ____________________

____

____

☐ ..... Foods he WILL NOT eat ____________________

____

____

☐ ..... Her dietary goals ____________________

____

☐ ..... His dietary goals ____________________

____

____

☐...... Exercise/sports she likes ____________________

____

☐...... Exercise/sports he likes ____________________

____

☐...... Time of day she prefers exercising ____________

____

☐...... Time of day he prefers exercising ____________

____

☐...... Her exercise goals ____________________

____

☐...... His exercise goals ____________________

____

The question below isn't just which gym; it's running in a gym versus in the neighborhood vs while walking the dog. Exercise for its own sake or as part of daily life?

☐...... Where she likes to exercise ____________________

____

☐...... Where he likes to exercise ____________________

____

____

Financial Planning

☐☐. Write wills ____________________________

☐☐. Write Advance Health Care Directives______

☐☐. Make copies and leave them with trusted family member ____________________________

☐☐. Update insurance beneficiary information __

☐☐ . Work policy____________________

His Policy Number __________________________

Her Policy Number __________________________

☐☐ . Non-work policy ________________

His Policy Number __________________________

Her Policy Number __________________________

☐☐. Take out life insurance if you don't have any.

☐ ..... Buy a fire safe box; put critical documents in.

☐☐ . Will ____________________________

☐☐ . Birth Certificate, incl. for children ____

☐☐ . Passport, SSN card, incl. for children _

☐☐ . Insurance policy __________________

☐☐ . Photos, etc., as proof for insurance ___

☐☐ . Other __________________________

☐ ..... $......... His retirement income______________

☐ ..... $......... Her retirement income _____________

☐...... $.........Combined retirement income ________

☐...... $.........Shortage from where you need/want to be ________________________________

☐...... $.........His monthly change in retirement savings ________________________________

____

☐...... $.........Her monthly change in retirement savings ________________________________

____

☐...... Goal year for purchasing a home ___________

☐...... Steps needed to achieve this _______________

____

☐...... $.........Amount saved toward down-payment

☐...... $.........Amount now in non-retirement investments ________________________________

☐...... $.........Amount desired in non-retirement investments (type desired?) ________________

☐...... $.........His monthly change in non-retirement Investments.________________________________

☐...... $.........Her monthly change in non-retirement investments ________________________

Existing Finances / Bills to Pay / Budget

Fill in the approximate amount of each bill, if you know, and which one of you will pay it each month.

☐ ..... $.........Gas Company ____________________

☐ ..... $.........Water and electric _________________

☐ ..... $.........Septic/trash_______________________

☐ ..... $.........Security system____________________

☐ ..... $.........Home Care Service – pool, maid, lawn

☐ ..... $.........Telephone (home) _________________

☐☐. $.........Cell phones _______________________

☐ ..... $.........Cable TV _________________________

☐☐. $.........Car insurance _____________________

☐ ..... $.........Homeowners/renters insurance _____

☐ ..... $.........Engagement ring insurance _________

☐ ..... $.........Her retirement investments (401K,

IRA) ____

☐ ..... $.........His retirement investments (401K,

IRA) ____

☐ ..... $.........Her investments (non-retirement)____

☐ ..... $.........His investments (non-retirement) ____

☐ ..... $.........Her subscriptions__________________

☐...... $.........His subscriptions ____________________

☐☐. $.........Newspapers ____________________

☐...... $.........Mortgage ____________________

☐...... $.........Her credit cards ____________________

☐...... $.........His credit cards ____________________

☐...... $.........Her student loans ____________________

☐...... $.........His student loans ____________________

☐...... $.........Her other loans/debts ____________________

☐...... $.........His other loans/debts ____________________

☐...... $.........Entertainment (movies, dvds, books) _

☐...... $.........Her lunch at work ____________________

☐...... $.........His lunch at work ____________________

☐...... $.........Other eating out ____________________

☐...... $.........Groceries ____________________

☐...... $.........Bottled water/other drinks ____________________

☐...... $.........Home repairs ____________________

☐...... $.........Other ____________________

☐...... $.........Her monthly income ____________________

☐...... $.........His monthly income ____________________

☐...... $.........Her money left after bill paying ______

☐...... $.........His money left after bill paying ______

Spending / Saving

When you think about Big Ticket Items, remember to include furniture, tools, major appliances, cars, a house.

$........ Her total existing debts (from previous pg)

$........ His total existing debts (from previous pg)

$........ Her total existing assets (from previous pg)

$........ His total existing assets (from previous pg)

$........ Combined existing debts ________________

$........ Combined existing assets ________________

____

☐ ..... Her just-for-fun spending ________________

____

☐ ..... His just-for-fun spending ________________

____

☐ ..... Big Ticket Items she really wants to save for _

____

____

☐ ..... Big Ticket Items he really wants to save for __

____

____

☐...... Things she is willing to "waste" money on (eating out)______________________________

____

☐...... Things he is willing to "waste" money on

(magazines) ______________________________

____

☐...... Her "necessary indulgences" (Starbucks)____

____

☐...... His "necessary indulgences" (fancy barber)__

____

☐...... Items she collects ______________________

____

☐...... Items he collects _______________________

____

☐...... How many years she keeps cars for________

☐...... How many years he keeps cars for ________

☐...... Her current car and anticipated replacement (type of car and how long from now) ____________

☐...... His current car and anticipated replacement (type of car and how long from now) ____________

____

Existing Accounts

Put the balance and limits for each account below to get an idea of your current financial situation. You must also decide if you will have individual or joint accounts.

☐ ..... His Checking Accounts (add spouse):

$ .... ☐ ______________________

$ .... ☐ ______________________

$ .... ☐ Business ______________________

☐ ..... Her Checking Accounts (add spouse):

$ .... ☐ ______________________

$ .... ☐ ______________________

$ .... ☐ Business ______________________

☐ ..... His Credit Cards (add spouse):

$ .... ☐ ______________________

$ .... ☐ ______________________

$ .... ☐ ______________________

$ .... ☐☐ Store Cards ______________________

$ .... ☐☐ Store Cards ______________________

____

☐ ..... Her Credit Cards (add spouse):

$ .... ☐ ______________________

$........ ☐ ______________________________

$........ ☐ ______________________________

$........ ☐☐ Store Cards ____________________

$........ ☐☐ Store Cards ____________________

____

☐...... His Investments (add spouse):

$........ ☐ Ira ___________________________

$........ ☐ 401K _________________________

$........ ☐ Other_________________________

____

☐...... Her Investments (add spouse):

$........ ☐ Ira ___________________________

$........ ☐ 401K _________________________

$........ ☐ Other_________________________

____

☐☐. Car payments ______________________

$........ ☐ His car________________________

$........ ☐ Her car _______________________

☐...... Monthly lease or mortgage (add spouse) ____

____

____

Where to Live / Ideal Home

If you don't know where you want to be, you can't get there.

☐ ..... Her family lives in ______________________

☐ ..... His family lives in ______________________

☐ ..... Her ideal distance from her family _________

____

☐ ..... His ideal distance from his family__________

____

☐ ..... Her minimum distance from his family _____

____

☐ ..... His minimum distance from her family _____

____

☐ ..... Her location preference (big city, town, state)

____

☐ ..... His location preference (climate, hilly vs. flat)

____

☐ ..... Her location restrictions (job in certain areas)

____

____

☐...... His location restrictions (health problems)___

____

☐...... Her goal year for purchasing home ________

____

☐...... His goal year for purchasing home ________

____

☐...... Her goal size for first home _____________

____

☐...... His goal size for first home _____________

____

☐...... Her goal for type of first home (condo?)_____

____

____

☐...... His goal for type of first home (townhouse?)_

____

____

☐...... Her goal location for first home __________

____

☐...... His goal location for first home __________

____

Moving In Together

☐ ..... Rent storage unit (If you can't agree on what is junk - store it. Work on reducing your collection of college lecture notes later.)

- ☐ ...... Facility name ____________________
- ☐ ...... Address ____________________
- ☐ ...... Phone number ____________________
- ☐ ...... Size and cost ____________________

☐☐. Plan for household goods to keep/toss. NO UNILATERAL DECISIONS. Maybe that wagon wheel coffee table has been in the family since they Brought The Wagon West - and can be hidden. ____

____

____

☐☐. Send move-out notice ____________________

☐ ..... Sign new lease/update current lease ________

☐☐. Submit change of address to post office _____

☐ ..... Name for telephone listing/unlisted ________

☐☐. Disconnect old utilities on ________________

- ☐☐ . Gas ____________________
- ☐☐ . Water and electric ____________________
- ☐☐ . Security system ____________________
- ☐☐ . Telephone (cell and home) __________

☐☐ .Cable ______________________

☐☐ .Septic/trash ________________

☐...... Personal space for each person ____________

☐...... New utilities connected in name of ________

starting on ______________________________

☐ ......Gas ________________________

☐ ......Water and electric ______________

☐ ......Security system ________________

☐ ......Telephone (cell and home) ________

☐ ......Cable ______________________

☐ ......Septic/trash __________________

☐...... Reserve rental truck ________________

☐...... Moving helpers ____________________

☐...... Confirm movers ___________________

☐☐. Update address with:

☐☐ .Insurance company ____________

☐☐ .DMV, employer ______________

☐☐ .Investment companies (IRA, 401K) ___

☐☐ .Magazine, CD/book clubs ________

☐☐ .Newspaper subscriptions (cancel one? New paper for a new city?) ____________

☐☐ .Banks, credit card companies _______

☐☐ :Student and other loans __________

Religion / Kids / Family

☐ ..... Religion he was raised____________________

☐ ..... Religion she was raised____________________

☐ ..... Religion he is now ____________________

☐ ..... Religion she is now ____________________

☐ ..... How religious he is ____________________

____

☐ ..... How religious she is ____________________

____

☐ ..... Important religious holidays to him ________

____

☐ ..... Important religious holidays to her________

____

☐ ..... Religion he wants to raise kids ___________

☐ ..... Religion she wants to raise kids___________

☐ ..... Religious education he wants for kids ______

____

☐ ..... Religious education she wants for kids _____

____

☐ ..... He wants #_____ of kids in about _____years

☐...... She wants #_____ of kids in about ____years

☐...... How often he wants to visit his family ______

☐...... How often she wants to visit her family _____

☐...... How often he needs to visit his family ______

☐...... How often she needs to visit her family _____

☐...... How many years can his parents be expected to live alone, unassisted? Where will they live after that and who will care for them? ________________

____

☐...... How many years can her parents be expected to live alone, unassisted? Where will they live after that and who will care for them? ________________

____

☐...... Does he have any other relatives that could end up your joint responsibility? (Younger siblings, nephews, or nieces he becomes guardian of, if they're orphaned.) ___________________________

____

☐...... Does she have any other relatives that could end up your joint responsibility? (Family that is elderly, infirm or has severe handicaps.) _________

____

____

Holidays / Special Days

This space is to record special holiday traditions you want to keep (or not!), how big (and expensive) you want them to be, and where you want to spend them (e.g., who will you see on Thanksgiving Day – or do you stay home?).

☐ ..... His birthday ______________________________

____

☐ ..... Her birthday ______________________________

____

☐ ..... Children's birthdays ______________________

____

☐ ..... Wedding anniversary ______________________

☐ ..... Yom Kippur ______________________________

____

☐ ..... Valentine's Day ___________________________

☐ ..... Passover__________________________________

____

☐ ..... Easter ___________________________________

____

☐ ..... Memorial Day______________________________

☐ ..... 4th of July _______________________________

☐...... Labor Day ______________________

☐...... Halloween ______________________

____

☐...... Thanksgiving ______________________

____

☐...... Black Friday ______________________

☐...... Chanukah ______________________

____

☐...... Christmas Eve ______________________

____

☐...... Christmas Day ______________________

____

☐...... Christmas Night ______________________

____

☐...... Day after Christmas ______________________

____

☐...... New Year's Eve ______________________

____

☐...... New Year's Day ______________________

____

Traditions (Hers, His, Ours)

☐ ..... Birthdays ______________________________

____

____

☐ ..... Anniversaries __________________________

____

____

☐ ..... Passover / Easter _______________________

____

____

____

☐ ..... Memorial Day / 4th of July / Labor Day ____

____

____

☐ ..... Halloween ______________________________

____

____

☐ ..... Thanksgiving (incl. the weekend) _________

____

☐...... Christmas / Chanukah ____________________

____

____

☐...... New Years ______________________________

____

____

☐...... Spring _________________________________

____

____

☐...... Summer ________________________________

____

____

☐...... Fall ___________________________________

____

____

☐...... Winter _________________________________

____

☐...... Other __________________________________

____

Table Assignments

Number of guests per table is ______.

Table #1

Guest #1 ____________________________________

Guest #2 ____________________________________

Guest #3 ____________________________________

Guest #4 ____________________________________

Guest #5 ____________________________________

Guest #6 ____________________________________

Guest #7 ____________________________________

Guest #8 ____________________________________

Guest #9 ____________________________________

Guest #10 ___________________________________

Table #2

Guest #1 ____________________________________

Guest #2 ____________________________________

Guest #3 ____________________________________

Guest #4 ____________________________________

Guest #5 ____________________________________

Guest #6 ____________________________________

Guest #7 ____________________________________

Guest #8 ____________________________________

Guest #9 ____________________________________

Guest #10 ___________________________________

Table #3

Guest #1 ____________________________________

Guest #2 ____________________________________

Guest #3 ____________________________________

Guest #4 ____________________________________

Guest #5 ____________________________________

Guest #6 ____________________________________

Guest #7 ____________________________________

Guest #8 ____________________________________

Guest #9 ____________________________________

Guest #10 ___________________________________

Table #4

Guest #1 ____________________________________

Guest #2 ____________________________________

Guest #3______________________________

Guest #4______________________________

Guest #5______________________________

Guest #6______________________________

Guest #7______________________________

Guest #8______________________________

Guest #9______________________________

Guest #10_____________________________

Table #5

Guest #1______________________________

Guest #2______________________________

Guest #3______________________________

Guest #4______________________________

Guest #5______________________________

Guest #6______________________________

Guest #7______________________________

Guest #8______________________________

Guest #9______________________________

Guest #10_____________________________

Table #6

Guest #1 ________________________________

Guest #2 ________________________________

Guest #3 ________________________________

Guest #4 ________________________________

Guest #5 ________________________________

Guest #6 ________________________________

Guest #7 ________________________________

Guest #8 ________________________________

Guest #9 ________________________________

Guest #10 _______________________________

Table #7

Guest #1 ________________________________

Guest #2 ________________________________

Guest #3 ________________________________

Guest #4 ________________________________

Guest #5 ________________________________

Guest #6 ________________________________

Guest #7 ________________________________

Guest #8______________________________

Guest #9______________________________

Guest #10_____________________________

Table #8

Guest #1______________________________

Guest #2______________________________

Guest #3______________________________

Guest #4______________________________

Guest #5______________________________

Guest #6______________________________

Guest #7______________________________

Guest #8______________________________

Guest #9______________________________

Guest #10_____________________________

Table #9

Guest #1______________________________

Guest #2______________________________

Guest #3______________________________

Guest #4______________________________

Guest #5 ______________________________

Guest #6 ______________________________

Guest #7 ______________________________

Guest #8 ______________________________

Guest #9 ______________________________

Guest #10 ______________________________

Table #10

Guest #1 ______________________________

Guest #2 ______________________________

Guest #3 ______________________________

Guest #4 ______________________________

Guest #5 ______________________________

Guest #6 ______________________________

Guest #7 ______________________________

Guest #8 ______________________________

Guest #9 ______________________________

Guest #10 ______________________________

Table #11

Guest #1 ______________________________

Guest #2________________________________

Guest #3________________________________

Guest #4________________________________

Guest #5________________________________

Guest #6________________________________

Guest #7________________________________

Guest #8________________________________

Guest #9________________________________

Guest #10_______________________________

Table #12

Guest #1________________________________

Guest #2________________________________

Guest #3________________________________

Guest #4________________________________

Guest #5________________________________

Guest #6________________________________

Guest #7________________________________

Guest #8________________________________

Guest #9________________________________

Guest #10 ______________________________

Table #13

Guest #1 ______________________________

Guest #2 ______________________________

Guest #3 ______________________________

Guest #4 ______________________________

Guest #5 ______________________________

Guest #6 ______________________________

Guest #7 ______________________________

Guest #8 ______________________________

Guest #9 ______________________________

Guest #10 ______________________________

Table #14

Guest #1 ______________________________

Guest #2 ______________________________

Guest #3 ______________________________

Guest #4 ______________________________

Guest #5 ______________________________

Guest #6 ______________________________

Guest #7________________________________

Guest #8________________________________

Guest #9________________________________

Guest #10_______________________________

Table #15

Guest #1________________________________

Guest #2________________________________

Guest #3________________________________

Guest #4________________________________

Guest #5________________________________

Guest #6________________________________

Guest #7________________________________

Guest #8________________________________

Guest #9________________________________

Guest #10_______________________________

Table #16

Guest #1________________________________

Guest #2________________________________

Guest #3________________________________

Guest #4 ________________________________

Guest #5 ________________________________

Guest #6 ________________________________

Guest #7 ________________________________

Guest #8 ________________________________

Guest #9 ________________________________

Guest #10 ________________________________

Table #17

Guest #1 ________________________________

Guest #2 ________________________________

Guest #3 ________________________________

Guest #4 ________________________________

Guest #5 ________________________________

Guest #6 ________________________________

Guest #7 ________________________________

Guest #8 ________________________________

Guest #9 ________________________________

Guest #10 ________________________________

Table #18

Guest #1______________________________

Guest #2______________________________

Guest #3______________________________

Guest #4______________________________

Guest #5______________________________

Guest #6______________________________

Guest #7______________________________

Guest #8______________________________

Guest #9______________________________

Guest #10_____________________________

Table #19

Guest #1______________________________

Guest #2______________________________

Guest #3______________________________

Guest #4______________________________

Guest #5______________________________

Guest #6______________________________

Guest #7______________________________

Guest #8 ________________________________

Guest #9 ________________________________

Guest #10 _______________________________

Table #20

Guest #1 ________________________________

Guest #2 ________________________________

Guest #3 ________________________________

Guest #4 ________________________________

Guest #5 ________________________________

Guest #6 ________________________________

Guest #7 ________________________________

Guest #8 ________________________________

Guest #9 ________________________________

Guest #10 _______________________________

Engagement and Shower Gift Recorder

When you've sent a thank-you note, check the box. For monetary gifts, write what you used the money for.

☐ ____

☐ ____

☐ ____

☐ ____

☐ ____

☐ ____

☐ ____

☐ ____

☐ ____

☐ ____

☐ ____

☐ ____

☐ ____

☐ ____

☐ ____

- [ ] ______
- [ ] ______
- [ ] ______
- [ ] ______
- [ ] ______
- [ ] ______
- [ ] ______
- [ ] ______
- [ ] ______
- [ ] ______
- [ ] ______
- [ ] ______
- [ ] ______
- [ ] ______
- [ ] ______
- [ ] ______
- [ ] ______
- [ ] ______
- [ ] ______

- [ ] ____________________
- [ ] ____________________
- [ ] ____________________
- [ ] ____________________
- [ ] ____________________
- [ ] ____________________
- [ ] ____________________
- [ ] ____________________
- [ ] ____________________
- [ ] ____________________
- [ ] ____________________
- [ ] ____________________
- [ ] ____________________
- [ ] ____________________
- [ ] ____________________
- [ ] ____________________
- [ ] ____________________
- [ ] ____________________
- [ ] ____________________

Wedding Gift Recorder

When you've sent a thank-you note, check the box. For monetary gifts, write what you used the money for.

- [ ] ______________________________
- [ ] ______________________________
- [ ] ______________________________
- [ ] ______________________________
- [ ] ______________________________
- [ ] ______________________________
- [ ] ______________________________
- [ ] ______________________________
- [ ] ______________________________
- [ ] ______________________________
- [ ] ______________________________
- [ ] ______________________________
- [ ] ______________________________
- [ ] ______________________________
- [ ] ______________________________
- [ ] ______________________________

- [ ] ______
- [ ] ______
- [ ] ______
- [ ] ______
- [ ] ______
- [ ] ______
- [ ] ______
- [ ] ______
- [ ] ______
- [ ] ______
- [ ] ______
- [ ] ______
- [ ] ______
- [ ] ______
- [ ] ______
- [ ] ______
- [ ] ______
- [ ] ______
- [ ] ______

- [ ] ____
- [ ] ____
- [ ] ____
- [ ] ____
- [ ] ____
- [ ] ____
- [ ] ____
- [ ] ____
- [ ] ____
- [ ] ____
- [ ] ____
- [ ] ____
- [ ] ____
- [ ] ____
- [ ] ____
- [ ] ____
- [ ] ____
- [ ] ____
- [ ] ____

- [ ] ____________________
- [ ] ____________________
- [ ] ____________________
- [ ] ____________________
- [ ] ____________________
- [ ] ____________________
- [ ] ____________________
- [ ] ____________________
- [ ] ____________________
- [ ] ____________________
- [ ] ____________________
- [ ] ____________________
- [ ] ____________________
- [ ] ____________________
- [ ] ____________________
- [ ] ____________________
- [ ] ____________________
- [ ] ____________________
- [ ] ____________________

- [ ] ____________________
- [ ] ____________________
- [ ] ____________________
- [ ] ____________________
- [ ] ____________________
- [ ] ____________________
- [ ] ____________________
- [ ] ____________________
- [ ] ____________________
- [ ] ____________________
- [ ] ____________________
- [ ] ____________________
- [ ] ____________________
- [ ] ____________________
- [ ] ____________________
- [ ] ____________________
- [ ] ____________________
- [ ] ____________________
- [ ] ____________________

- [ ] ______
- [ ] ______
- [ ] ______
- [ ] ______
- [ ] ______
- [ ] ______
- [ ] ______
- [ ] ______
- [ ] ______
- [ ] ______
- [ ] ______
- [ ] ______
- [ ] ______
- [ ] ______
- [ ] ______
- [ ] ______
- [ ] ______
- [ ] ______
- [ ] ______

Notes

About the Author

Liz Long and her husband have been happily married for quite a while now. Their wedding was fun for everyone, but not really expensive, as these things go. The big shocker was that the bridesmaids could actually wear their dresses again - no joke.

Liz and her husband had a great vacation on their honeymoon. They didn't go to a single beach, but that's not their ideal vacation.

Her other books include The Constitution: It's the OS for the US, Leader of the Pack: An Introduction to Cub Scouts, and OMG! Not the Zombies!

Contact the Author

You can connect with Liz through:

Email - Liz@LizLongAuthor.com

Facebook - LizLongAuthor

Goodreads - Liz Long (the one wearing a hat)

Pinterest - LizLongAuthor

Twitter - @LizLongAuthor

Because Amazon reviews really do matter, especially for indie authors, please take a few minutes and post a review on Amazon.com.

18765990R00131

Made in the USA
Middletown, DE
20 March 2015